# The Service-Oriented Enterprise

## Learn Enterprise Architecture and Its Viable Services

**Tom Graves**

Apress®

*The Service-Oriented Enterprise: Learn Enterprise Architecture and Its Viable Services*

Tom Graves
Tetradian Consulting, Eaglehawk, VIC, Australia

ISBN-13 (pbk): 978-1-4842-9188-7      ISBN-13 (electronic): 978-1-4842-9189-4
https://doi.org/10.1007/978-1-4842-9189-4

Managing Director, Apress Media LLC: Welmoed Spahr
Acquisitions Editor: Aditee Mirashi
Development Editor: James Markham
Coordinating Editor: Aditee Mirashi

Cover designed by eStudioCalamar

Cover image by Jason Leung on Unsplash (www.unsplash.com)

Distributed to the book trade worldwide by Apress Media, LLC, 1 New York Plaza, New York, NY 10004, U.S.A. Phone 1-800-SPRINGER, fax (201) 348-4505, e-mail orders-ny@springer-sbm.com, or visit www.springeronline.com. Apress Media, LLC is a California LLC and the sole member (owner) is Springer Science + Business Media Finance Inc (SSBM Finance Inc). SSBM Finance Inc is a **Delaware** corporation.

For information on translations, please e-mail booktranslations@springernature.com; for reprint, paperback, or audio rights, please e-mail bookpermissions@springernature.com.

Apress titles may be purchased in bulk for academic, corporate, or promotional use. eBook versions and licenses are also available for most titles. For more information, reference our Print and eBook Bulk Sales web page at http://www.apress.com/bulk-sales.

Any source code or other supplementary material referenced by the author in this book is available to readers on GitHub (https://github.com/Apress). For more detailed information, please visit http://www.apress.com/source-code.

Printed on acid-free paper

# Table of Contents

# About the Author

 **Tom Graves** has been an independent consultant for more than four decades in business transformation, enterprise architecture, and knowledge management. His clients in Europe, Australasia, and the Americas cover a broad range of industries including small-businesses, banking, utilities, manufacturing, logistics, engineering, media, telecoms, research, defense, and government. He has a special interest in whole-enterprise architectures for nonprofit, social, government, and commercial enterprises.

# About the Technical Reviewers

**Daljit Banger** has 38 years of IT industry experience, having undertaken assignments in locations across the globe, including the United Kingdom, the United States, Sweden, Switzerland, Finland, Hong Kong, and Brazil, to name a few, on behalf of large, multinational companies. Daljit has successfully managed several large professional teams of architects, has contributed to several publications, and is the author of several freeware software products for enterprise architecture. Daljit holds a master of science (MSc) degree, is a Chartered IT Fellow of the British Computer Society (BCS), and chairs the BCS Enterprise Architecture Specialist Group.

**Darryl Carr** is a consulting Enterprise Architect at Perth-based consultancy JourneyOne, with over 30 years of experience helping organizations. Darryl is also the editor of the *Enterprise Architecture Professional Journal* and passionate supporter of the global EA community through involvement in events and forums such as the BIL-T Conference Series and Women in Architecture.

# Acknowledgments

Among others, the following people kindly provided comments and feedback on the early drafts of this book: Daljit Banger (GB), Shawn Callahan (AU), Charles Edwards (GB), Geoff Elliott (GB), Nigel Green (GB), Charles Millar (GB), Kim Parker (AU), Liz Poraj-Wilczynska (GB), Peter Tseglakof (AU), Jaco Vermeulen (GB).

Please note that, to preserve commercial and personal confidentiality, the stories and examples in this book have often been adapted, combined, and in part fictionalized from experiences in a variety of contexts, and do not and are not intended to represent any specific individual or organization.

All registered trademarks such as Zachman, TOGAF, FEAF, ITIL, ASL, BiSL, etc., are acknowledged as the intellectual property of the respective owners.

# Introduction

Everything in the enterprise is a service. Everything the enterprise does is a service. Everything the enterprise delivers is a service – even products are services, in a sense. And the enterprise itself is a service. *Everything* is a service.

That's the key idea behind the *service-oriented enterprise*: a view of the enterprise in which everything is seen in terms of services and their interactions and interdependencies, providing consistency and simplicity everywhere, and creating new space for agility and innovation in the enterprise.

This book explores why and how to put that idea into practice, with real business benefits across the entire enterprise.

## Who Should Read This Book?

The book is intended for enterprise architects and others who deal with the practical implications of whole-of-enterprise issues.

It should also be useful for strategists, service-managers, decision-makers, and influencers, and also for anyone who works with "pervasive" themes such as supply-chains, value-webs, quality, security, knowledge-sharing, business ethics and social responsibility, health, safety, and environment.

# What's in This Book?

The text is divided into three main parts:

- *Part 1: Basics – An Overview*: Reviewing key terms such as "enterprise architecture" and "service-oriented architecture," and the core metaphors underlying the service-oriented enterprise

- *Part 2: Principles – An Overview*: Describing core ideas about the structure and relationships between services, and their relationship to the structure of the enterprise

- *Part 3: Practice – An Overview*: Illustrating how to apply the principles in real-world business contexts, using a Functional Business Model as the anchor for the enterprise service map, process tree, costing model, and other variants

Each part contains several chapters, as smaller chunks to apply straightaway in your day-to-day work. Although there's a fair amount of theory, the keyword here is *practice*: the aim is to give you something that you can *use*.

So each chapter includes examples and stories to place the ideas into a real-life context, with references to other relevant resources. Most chapters include an "Into Practice" section, with questions to help you apply the material within your own context. At the end of the book, there's also a glossary, which should help in clarifying the broader meaning of some of the common terms used in the architecture of the service-oriented enterprise, and a "Resources" section, pointing to sources for further information.

But first, what *is* the service-oriented enterprise? To answer that, we need to explore some basic terms such as "enterprise architecture" and "service-oriented architecture" and the underlying metaphors that we use to describe the enterprise.

# One Last Note Before We Begin

There are a handful of images in this book that had to be reduced in size to fit the book, and may be difficult to read. We've made full-size versions available for download at `github.com/apress-service-oriented-enterprise`.

# PART I

# Basics – An Overview

Before we get into the meat of the issues, there are a few background items we need to address.

One of these is the role of enterprise architecture, which we'll explore in Chapter 1, "Basics – Enterprise Architecture." At present, this field is often regarded as a subset of IT, and specifically of IT governance. But it makes far more sense if we extend it outward to its more literal meaning as the architecture of the enterprise as a whole.

Enterprise architecture is about the structure and story of the enterprise – how everything fits together in support of the enterprise vision, values, and goals. Viewing an enterprise entirely in terms of services is one of the more valuable ways to assess that structure, especially as it provides consistency between every part and every level within the enterprise.

A service-oriented architecture also starts to make more sense from that point of view, as we'll see in Chapter 2, "Basics – Service-Oriented Architecture." As with enterprise-architecture, it initially arose as a way to resolve issues around detail-level IT, but here we expand its scope outward, as an architectural style to understand the entire enterprise in terms of service structures and content and their mutual interactions and interdependencies.

As part of this, we'll also need to introduce some basic themes and terminology from formal systems-theory. This still isn't well-known in business as yet: unfortunate but understandable, because much of "hard-systems theory" is described in a complex, arcane mathematics that may well seem impenetrable – and, frankly, irrelevant – to most people in business. The type we need here, though, is the human-oriented "soft-systems" approach, which is much more approachable, and more easily expressed in business terms for the real business context.

Beneath that distinction between "hard-systems" and "soft-systems" is a fundamental difference in the underlying metaphor, in the overall way we describe the enterprise. We'll explore this in Chapter 3, "Basics – A Matter of Metaphor." There's a key contrast here between the notion of "enterprise as a machine" – probably *the* most common business metaphor since the days of "scientific management," in the early part of the twentieth century – and the more recent concept of "enterprise as living organism." The mechanistic view has some real value at the detail-level of technology and process-design, but it simply does not work when we try to apply it to the whole enterprise – as many business-folk have discovered the hard way, in expensive debacles such as the failure of so many attempts at IT-centered "business process reengineering." Instead, if we are to gain the full value from a service-oriented architecture, we need to shift toward the more holistic, all-encompassing view of the "living enterprise" model.

# CHAPTER 1

# Basics – Enterprise Architecture

What *is* the enterprise? What holds it together? What structures do we need to make it work better, to help it adapt to its changing circumstances and business environment?

These are the core questions underlying the formal discipline of enterprise architecture. It's still a relatively new discipline: the term itself was coined only a few decades ago, building on previous ideas about "information systems architecture" and the like. There are several standards and formats – TOGAF (The Open Group Architecture Framework), FEAF (US Federal Enterprise Architecture Framework), and the Zachman framework being some of the best-known examples. This leads us, though, to ask: What *is* an "enterprise"? For that matter, what is meant by "architecture" in this context?

In every form of architecture – building architecture, naval architecture, process architecture, business architecture, whatever – the real focus is on structure, and the *use* of that structure. In the architecture and design of a hospital, for example, we would be as concerned with the workflows and other usage-patterns *within* the hospital as its physical framework of walls and wiring, passageways, and plumbing. The same is true of enterprise architecture: it's about structure – *any* kind of structure within the enterprise, from data-definitions to downpipes and dumper-trucks – and the principles and guidelines that govern the *use* of that structure.

© Tom Graves 2023
T. Graves, *The Service-Oriented Enterprise*, https://doi.org/10.1007/978-1-4842-9189-4_1

So what then is an enterprise? According to the FEAF specification, it's any kind of entity "supporting a defined business scope and mission" within which the various members or components "must coordinate their functions and share information" to achieve that purpose. Perhaps more generally, we might think of an enterprise as a collective human endeavor – a shared story that drives action. In that latter sense, the "enterprise" might be a commercial business; it might be government or nonprofit; it might be the local football club or the village New Mothers group; it actually doesn't matter what the size or purpose might be, as long as there is a defined scope and mission to share.

---

There's an important catch here about which we do need to be aware. In colloquial usage, "organization" and "enterprise" are often considered to be the same thing: an organization is an enterprise, and an enterprise is an organization. Yet in architectural terms, there are some fundamental differences between "organization" and "enterprise": an organization is a legal entity bounded by rules, roles, and responsibilities, whereas an enterprise is more an emotive construct bounded by vision, values, and commitments. Their boundaries *can* coincide, of course, but that isn't always the case: for example, when we need to talk about supply-chain or market, we'll be dealing with an enterprise that by definition *must* be broader than the organization. In effect, the "enterprise" provides the *context* for whatever aspect of the organization we're addressing at that time, and in essence, in enterprise architecture, we create an architecture *for* an organization *about* the enterprise that provides its context.

To keep things simple, I'll generally use "the enterprise" here in that colloquial sense, that it's sort of the same as "the organization." Just be aware that they're not *actually* the same at all, and that in few places that difference will matter. I'll highlight those when we get there.

---

Although an organization is a kind of enterprise, not every enterprise is delimited by the legal and other boundaries of an organization. *An enterprise may be any subset or superset of the organization*: the IT department is an enterprise in its own right, within the overall enterprise of the parent organization; a multipartner cross-industry consortium is likewise an enterprise made up of a shared "mission and scope" to which a group of smaller enterprises choose to align. There's no inherent restriction there, and in some cases, the effective boundaries of the enterprise may well change from minute to minute.

Under those circumstances, governance of the enterprise can get complicated, to say the least. This is where enterprise architecture comes into the picture:

- **Enterprise architecture is a discipline through which an enterprise can identify, develop, and maintain its knowledge of and choices about its purpose, its structure, its story, and itself.**

Enterprise architecture identifies and monitors the structures and more that are needed to support that shared mission; it assists in managing change and responses to change; it provides guidance and consistency across the whole scope.

But here we may hit up against a problem of divergence between what is commonly thought to be the scope of enterprise architecture and the real scope it needs to have. We need to address that issue of scope before we can move on.

# The Scope of Enterprise Architecture

In most current descriptions, "enterprise architecture" is associated almost entirely with IT – in effect, the term is a kind of shorthand for "enterprise-wide IT architecture." But with each new stage of maturity, the scope has needed to expand further, from low-level technology and interfaces to structures for data and applications and then to a somewhat belated recognition that all of this needed to be linked to and driven from business strategy.

Yet all of this is still centered solely on IT. Yes, there is a distinct and separate discipline of business-architecture that addresses business-models, process-flows, organizational structures, and so on, yet still far too often what's called "business-architecture" in the enterprise-architecture context is still little more just an IT-oriented summary of "anything not IT that might affect IT." So as shown in Figure 1-1, a typical view of the scope of that "enterprise architecture" would be as in the TOGAF specification.

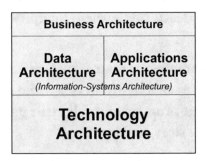

**Figure 1-1.**  *The IT architecture hierarchy*

---

Note the relative sizes of each area of interest in that diagram. Back in the original TOGAF methodology, for example, assessment of low-level technology was assigned more than six times as many development steps as for the whole of the rest of the business put together. Kind of an imbalance there…

---

Every enterprise is different, yet very few are as IT-centric as the standard enterprise-architecture models suggest. And for the rest? Perhaps the simplest way is to describe each enterprise in terms of four distinct dimensions, which we could summarize as the four classic ways an enterprise distinguishes itself from its competitors:

- *Through products and services*: A *physical* dimension of actions and transactions, "the way we do things round here"

- *Through knowledge and innovation*: A *conceptual* dimension of ideas and information, "what we know, how we think"

- *Through relationships and "feel"*: A *relational* dimension of people and their individual skills and experience, "how we relate with each other and with others"

- *Through vision and purpose*: An *aspirational* dimension about direction, focus, morale, belonging, "who we are and what we stand for"

The FEAF-reference-model describes these respectively as "Other Fixed Assets," "Technology" (by which they mean IT, though that's actually only a subset of knowledge-technology), "Human Capital," and "Business." These dimensions interweave as the distinct and distinctive nature of the enterprise as a whole. So if we were to reframe that classic model, the layering of a *real* whole-enterprise architecture would look more like as shown in Figure 1-2.

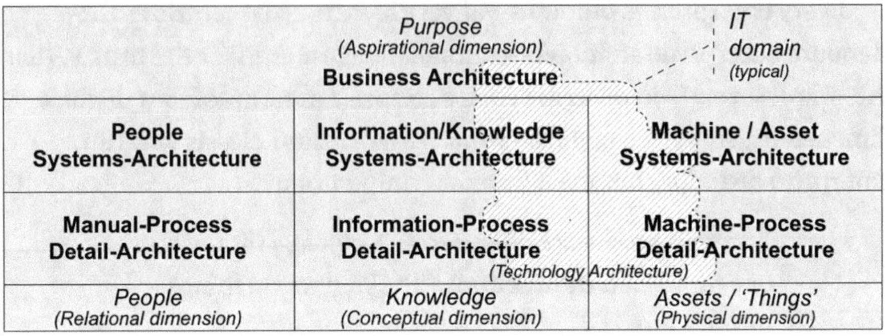

| Purpose *(Aspirational dimension)* **Business Architecture** | | IT domain *(typical)* |
|---|---|---|
| **People Systems-Architecture** | **Information/Knowledge Systems-Architecture** | **Machine / Asset Systems-Architecture** |
| **Manual-Process Detail-Architecture** | **Information-Process Detail-Architecture** | **Machine-Process Detail-Architecture** *(Technology Architecture)* |
| People *(Relational dimension)* | Knowledge *(Conceptual dimension)* | Assets / 'Things' *(Physical dimension)* |

***Figure 1-2.*** *Whole-of-enterprise structure*

So enterprise architecture can't be solely about IT, but about how *every* aspect of the enterprise interacts with everything else – including security, marketing, business-models, value-flows, and much, much more. And it also can't be centered on IT: in fact, it isn't centered anywhere, other than on that guiding theme, the "defined business scope and mission." In short

- **The scope of enterprise architecture is always the whole of the enterprise – the enterprise *as* a whole.**

We may choose, for practical reasons, to set suitable limits on the scope of an architectural assessment or design. But the moment we forget that that's an arbitrary choice, not a fact, we'd be in trouble straightaway: the real scope – *always* – is the whole of the enterprise.

# The Purpose of Enterprise Architecture

But what's the point of all of this? What's the *purpose* of enterprise architecture? To answer that, we could perhaps return to that FEAF definition earlier, that an enterprise has various members and components that coordinate their functions and share information to express or achieve their shared "mission" or vision. From that perspective, the architecture provides a means to support that process of coordination; it provides consistency across the whole of the enterprise scope and a consistent *description* of that scope.

That's where standard reference-frameworks come into the picture. For example, Open Group's "Integrated Information Infrastructure Reference Model" provides one such view for the IT industry, while eTOM and SID ("Enhanced Telecom Operations Map" and "Structured Information/ Data") provide the same kind of descriptions for telecommunications service providers, and SCOR (Supply-Chain Operations Reference-model) describes logistics and other supply chain services.

Yet these are all static models: they describe structure, but not much about *interactions* between the components of those structures. And they don't explain much about the *human* side of the systems – such as the "tacit knowledge" that resides only in people's heads and is most often shared through stories and action-based learning. For these, we need a broader view of the structure, the system, and the scope and the flows and interactions across all of those elements.

That's what a "services" view of the architecture can provide for us. Services present a consistent frame through which to understand a structure, and service-choreography describes the *use* of that structure, which leads us, in turn, to a service-oriented view of the enterprise as a whole – the *service-oriented enterprise.*

That in turn would depend on a view of "service-orientation" that's as broad as the scope of the enterprise itself. But as with "enterprise architecture," the term is at present strongly associated with IT alone – too strongly for our needs here. To make this work, we need first to take a detour to find the *real* meaning of "service-oriented architecture."

# Into Practice

- What are the bounds of "the enterprise" in your own business context? Are they a subset of the organization, synonymous with the organization, or do they extend beyond the organization itself? What are the dynamics of those bounds – in what ways do they change, and for what purposes?

- Does your organization maintain some kind of enterprise-architecture? If so, what is its current scope? Where within the organization does it reside? Who has responsibility for its scope and governance?

- If your existing enterprise-architecture is restricted to an IT-centric scope, what would need to be done to extend that to a true enterprise-wide scope? What can *you* do to assist in that change?

- What support does enterprise-architecture provide to enhance consistency across the enterprise? In what ways could that support be further enhanced within your enterprise?

# Summary

In this chapter, we explored the basics of enterprise architecture as a formal discipline. Historically, it had roots in IT systems and technology-management, but it has steadily extended its scope toward covering the whole enterprise – and it will need that much broader scope if it is to fully describe the requirements of the service-oriented enterprise. To support that need, we derived a definition of enterprise architecture as "a discipline through which an enterprise can identify, develop, and maintain its knowledge of and choices about its purpose, its structure, its story, and itself," and that its overall scope would always be the enterprise as a whole. The real value of enterprise architecture is that it supports consistency, reliability, and overall effectiveness for the organization as it undergoes any kind of change.

In the next chapter, we'll find out more about how enterprise architecture connects with service-oriented architectures.

# CHAPTER 2

# Basics – Service-Oriented Architecture

To me, a service is literally something that serves a need – hence, a service-oriented architecture is a way to guide the purpose, structure, story, and so on of all those things in the enterprise that serve a need. Yet if we read the existing literature on service-oriented architecture, we'll usually find much the same as we saw with enterprise architecture: it seems it's almost all about detail-level IT such as microservices, and very little else. As with enterprise architecture, though, that's not the whole story: the IT is only one small part of the enterprise and represents only a small part of its architecture, too. However, the IT is often the only part of the architecture that people know, so it's probably the best place to start; we just have to remember to translate any IT-centric assumptions to the broader whole-of-enterprise scope.

In IT-architecture, a *service* is a composite made up of small blocks of functionality that collectively present a unified interface – often but not always a single interface – to the "external" world, and are otherwise *autonomous*, ideally with no "hardwired" links to any other services. Some of the other key ideas include

© Tom Graves 2023
T. Graves, *The Service-Oriented Enterprise*, https://doi.org/10.1007/978-1-4842-9189-4_2

- *Loosely coupled*: Services have minimal dependence on each other; "services share schema and contract, not class," to quote one of the original services theorists, Don Box.

- *Contract-based*: The service to be delivered is defined in a "service description document" or some other kind of "contract" or service-level agreement.

- *Discoverable*: The service and its interface-contract – including information on the *quality* available in the contract, to aid process optimization – should be identifiable automatically.

- *Abstraction*: As long as the service delivers in accordance with the specified interface-contract, how it does what it does should be a "black box," internal detail that is (mostly) irrelevant to the user of the service.

- *Reusable* and *composable*: The service should be designed for reuse in a variety of different ways and in aggregations into larger blocks of shared functionality.

- *Interchangeable*: It should be possible to switch between services on different systems and from different service-providers that adhere to the same nominal service-contract specification.

Overall, this gives some great advantages:

- We break free from monolithic, hardwired "applications" that are cumbersome, fragile, and hard to change.

- Developers can optimize the internal mechanisms of a service without affecting its exposed interface.

- We can support "separation of concerns" to ensure that elements that do different things don't get bundled together and become difficult to change.

- We can "mix and match" between services to create new "mashups" for rapid response to business change.

- Services can be described in business terms, enabling people without an IT background to create their own personalized mashups.

- We can call on the facilities of multiple service-providers for the same nominal service, for load-balancing and risk-management, or for business reasons such as reduced costs or faster response.

All good, but there *are* some significant downsides, which at times may be overlooked amidst the flood of marketing-hype. There's a sense sometimes of a wishful attitude of "build it and they will come"; yet in a true service-oriented architecture, services have no inherent context, they just *are*. So issues around "discoverability" – self-advertising, in effect – suddenly become nontrivial: a concern that barely existed with the old monolithic applications, where every function was hardwired into the runtime code.

Also, unlike those monolithic applications, there's no inherent built-in mechanism that links services together into processes: that choreography has to come from somewhere beyond the services themselves. And the need for service-contracts can bring a hefty overhead in terms of bandwidth and execution-time, especially where service-connections need to be created in real-time.

A service-orientation for IT-architecture enables new options, new possibilities: one such example is cloud-computing, in which IT-services and storage can be exchanged and accessed from anywhere across the Web. Yet all of this is still solely from the IT perspective. Once we look wider and extend the scope of a service-oriented architecture, we start to see that there are other advantages, and other challenges – some of them subtle, even strange, perhaps, but all of which *do* need to be addressed.

# Security and Other Service Challenges

Probably the greatest challenges to a service-oriented architecture revolve around security. Every access to anything will require some kind of identity-management:

- Is this requester who they claim to be?

- If they are, do they have the appropriate "need to know, need to use"?

- If it's a commercial service, do they have access to the funds to pay for the service?

- How do we confirm all of this, within the response-time specified in the service-contract?

In a typical application, we would control access to information or functions via some kind of token. Once someone has logged in to some system, we can use that token to track anything they do and ask for within the bounds of that system, and respond accordingly. Often, all we'll need to do is something like a lookup to a list of passwords and a list of matching access-rights, and we'd be all but done: problem solved. For the enterprise as a whole, almost the only complications are perhaps the need to get people to change their passwords from time to time, to reduce the risk that security may be compromised, and also the need to align access-controls for the various different monolithic systems that people need to use – hence the "holy grail" of a so-called "single sign-on" across every system, which sounds simple enough in theory, if not so simple in practice...

But in a service-oriented model, identity-management is suddenly *much* more complicated – especially on the Internet, which has no built-in mechanism to track "stateful" concerns such as identity and security. "The system" – such as it is – consists of layer upon layer of near-arbitrary collections of "small pieces loosely joined": we can pass around a token, perhaps, but as yet there's no quick, simple, automatic means to link that token to any central register of access-rights. And once we're outside the enterprise firewall – as we would be with most cloud-computing services, for example – we have to deal with all the security nightmare of the Internet, with hacking, spoofing, interception, forged identity, and the rest. Even with VPNs (Virtual Private Networks) to help, it's not a pretty picture.

---

In practice, the technical challenges of SOA are almost trivial compared to its security challenges. The reason there is that many of the issues have little or nothing to do with IT – a fact which can be difficult for anyone who tries to tackle this with an IT-only background, a fixed IT-centric view of the business world, and an equally fixed assumption that every possible problem has an IT-based solution. But unless we *do* think wider about security than just the IT issues, we're likely to cause more problems than we solve: when security is our responsibility, we're responsible for *all* of it, not just the easy part that's within our comfort-zone!

---

Another classic problem in service-choreography is what's known as "deadly embrace." An example from the hardwired computer-systems of a few decades ago would be where one service gains exclusive access to a datastore and then requests the printer at the same time as another service locks the printer for its use and then requests the datastore. Each service is then stuck waiting for the other, which would not be popular with the services' users.

In principle, and in direct form, at least that kind of problem has long since been resolved with tactics such as asynchronous printer-queues and optimistic record-locking, and the sheer speed of most present-day data-processing also helps. But each service-transaction takes *time* to set up, especially through all those worldwide routing mechanisms of the Internet, and when we have to wade our way through layer upon layer of access-control services and suchlike to get anything done, the total setup time may well exceed that for the actual transaction many times over. And that's assuming that everything works: it's not always obvious what will happen when any service-transaction fails within an overall choreography. So even if it's not a true "deadly embrace" in a technical sense, it may well feel like it... And when such a widely distributed system fails in that way, it's often far from obvious as to whose responsibility it would be to fix it, which is guaranteed trouble at a business level. So cloud-computing may sound almost perfect in principle, perhaps, but may not be so perfect in practice.

And then there are a whole swathe of other issues that have little or nothing to do with IT as such, but can have serious impacts on IT-based services. For example, almost every country has its own distinct and different rules around privacy, record-keeping, and the like. So while in principle data could be stored anywhere in the world, many countries mandate that some (but *only* some) information should never cross national borders – which means that service-users must have proof from service-providers that that is indeed the case.

Other countries – particularly the United States – assert legal concerns about restricting information to their own citizens only – who may, however, be anywhere in the world. Then there are the thorny issues around pornography and the like, where access may be limited not by nationality but by age or other personal attributes. All of these lead to chaotic confusions about who can and can't see what, and who has authority and responsibility to control such limitations – let alone, again, dealing with all the hackers and spoofers and suchlike. Messy indeed.

A true service-oriented architecture needs to be able to deal with every one of these issues, which is not straightforward at all. This is why a service-based view of the enterprise needs also to be strongly linked to a solid structure for service-management – not just for IT but for the whole of the enterprise.

# Services and Service-Management

Whether in cloud-computing or in old-style applications, IT services need to be linked together into end-to-end business processes – which means there needs to be something above the services themselves to create that choreography. In the same way, there also needs to be an IT infrastructure on which the services will run. The latter would be more the realm of IT-architecture, perhaps, but all of this would come under the general heading of "service management."

Probably *the* international standard for IT-service management is ITIL, the "IT Infrastructure Library" developed by the UK Office of Government Commerce. So in this context, it's interesting to compare two versions of that standard: Version 2, published in 2004, and the Version 3 update, released in 2007.

---

The later Version 4 of ITIL, released in 2019, did kind of combine the two perspectives, but arguably recentered itself primarily around IT. For our purposes here, the difference in perspective between Versions 2 and 3 is the crucial distinction that we need here.

---

ITIL v2 uses a classic IT-centric "them and us" model for its overview. On the far left, there's "The Business"; on the far right, there's "The Technology." Between them sits the core of service-management, service delivery and service support, with an interface of "The Business

Perspective" on one side and ICT Infrastructure Management on the other. Above and below, we have a useful focus on planning, on application management, and on ever-essential security-management. That's it, apart from an emphasis throughout on "IT/business alignment" – though it's never very clear about who is supposed to align with whom.

ITIL v3 is radically different: there's almost no IT-centrism at all. In principle, it's all about service-management for IT, but apart from a few low-level technical details, we could remove the term "IT" throughout and it would still make perfect sense. It starts with service strategy, moves on to service design, then service transition about implementing those designs, and service operation. Interweaving all of those is continual service improvement. Each is "a set of specialized organizational capabilities for providing value to customers in the form of services," with an emphasis on managing the overall service life cycle as much as service delivery and support. And though never stated explicitly, perhaps the real key point in ITIL is this:

- **Service-management is itself a service: it delivers the services of service-management.**

The ITIL standard describes those service-management services and the *relationships* between those services, both in terms of their interdependencies and choreography and in terms of the mutual responsibilities over time. But it also helps us to think about services in much broader terms than those of IT architecture alone, which matters, because, ultimately, *everything* is a service.

# Everything Is a Service

Whatever it looks like, and whatever form it may take, *everything* in an enterprise delivers a service. That's the real implication of a service-oriented architecture and also the real reason for its importance to the enterprise.

Everything is a service. Even products are proto-services, in a sense, because they provide the end-customer with the means to deliver a self-service: a vacuum-cleaner provides the service of cleaned floors, the grocery-shopping provides the self-service of meals, and so on. "Customers do not buy products," says the ITIL v3 specification, "they buy the satisfaction of particular needs." And we satisfy those needs through the services we provide.

---

Shifting the perspective from products to services can be more profitable, too. Interface, Inc. is one of the world's leading manufacturers of flooring materials and, some three decades ago, in the words of its founder Ray Anderson, was consuming "an ocean of petroleum" each year to make its products. It was a profitable enterprise, if perhaps not as profitable as it could have been – though with the "business as usual" mindset of the time, it was far from clear as to what needed to change to make that quantum shift in profitability.

But in the late 1990s, Anderson had what he called "a spear to the chest" – a kind of double-epiphany about sustainability. One side of it was a recognition that every scrap of waste – at that time, a huge problem for the corporation – was something that they'd paid for but couldn't sell. Hence, zero-waste was not merely a "feel-good" goal, but a *business* matter with serious business impacts: waste-reduction leads directly to more profit, and *everyone* wins. At the present time, Interface is well on its way halfway toward its "Mission Zero" goal – zero waste, zero environmental impact, everything recycled – and its profitability continues to climb with each passing year.

Anderson's other "epiphany" was a realization about a link between products, services, and waste. Interface had sold carpet and other flooring *products*, but what its clients really wanted – "the satisfaction of a particular need" – was the *service* of covered floors, and to the end-customer, that service had higher value *as* a service. So Interface started to shift their business that way – and discovered that to make it work, they also had to shift their attitude to waste. When the company was oriented toward products, it was in their interest to get their customers to be careless about waste: more waste equals more product sold, and built-in obsolescence seems like a good idea, too. But it's the other way round when the company embeds the product in its own fixed-fee service; suddenly, it's in the company's interest for customers to *minimize* their waste, and for products to be as durable as possible. So for the service-oriented enterprise, sustainability is good business in every sense – and once again, *everyone* wins.

---

In IT service-oriented architecture, we rethink IT functions and the like in terms of services. But in the service-oriented enterprise, we take that idea a stage further, and rethink *everything* in service terms. Service-management is a service; management *itself* is a service; so is strategy, architecture, the office canteen. Everything in the entire enterprise is a service.

In ITIL v3, a service is defined in rather abstract terms, as a means of delivering value by facilitating the customer's desired outcomes. The service is both valued and valuable because we take on some of the complexity and risk on the customer's behalf. And the service is accorded a value by the customer to the extent that it makes those outcomes easier to achieve.

In terms of how value flows around the enterprise, a product is about the "what," whereas a service is more about the "how," "who," "where," and "when." But what the customer is *really* interested in is their "why" – and often doesn't greatly care about how that "why" can be achieved, as long as it *is* achieved with the minimum of difficulty and fuss. As a service-provider, that's *our* desired outcome: a satisfied customer. In a commercial context, satisfaction *matters* – because a satisfied customer is likely to come back for more.

---

Incidentally, this is one point where "black-box" encapsulation of service-internals may cross over with demands for transparency, giving a much more subtle definition of "customer satisfaction."

When the Australian "Ghan" railway line from Adelaide to Darwin was upgraded some years back, one of the tenders for the contract was presented by a Chinese consortium. Unlike the other tenders, which assumed a relatively small workforce and large amounts of heavy machinery, the Chinese proposed instead to use a vast manual workforce of *half a million* laborers. The delivered-service *results* would have been exactly the same, created to the same nominal service-level agreement. The Chinese proposal even worked out cheaper – even allowing for the logistics of serving that workforce in difficult near-desert conditions – hence would have been much "better" than the other tenders if the only deciding-criterion had been the price.

But an end-customer may well be concerned with more than just the end-result – and that was certainly true in this case. For a start, the politics of that proposal were *way* too scary – especially as that imported workforce would represent a significant percentage of the country's entire population. So sometimes the simple black-box encapsulation can risk *reducing* "customer satisfaction." In an IT service-oriented architecture, we might not need to take account of such issues, but at the whole-of-enterprise level, we certainly do.

Something else to think about, anyway.

---

In the service-oriented enterprise, every activity has an explicitly identified customer to whom that service has value, and each of those customers has an outcome that they want to achieve. Those two points *define* the service-need and hence the structure and nature of the service.

---

Perhaps more to the point, if we *can't* identify the customer and their need, we're at risk of delivering a service that has no perceived value. That's a situation that is far from uncommon in larger enterprises, particularly in the myriad of performance reports created with so much effort but that no-one ever actually reads…

Do beware, though, of the common mistake of attempting to define that value solely in monetary terms. We can't *eat* money; we can't travel with money alone; we can't get a hug from it, or a greeting home; it doesn't even make a good floor-covering. Money is a *means* to an outcome – not the outcome itself. To make a service-oriented architecture work, we need to be clear about what that outcome is – not just the means by which we get there.

---

Products enable services, and services in turn enable outcomes. As a service-provider, delivery of the service is the endpoint of all our work, but from the customer's perspective, the service is only a means to an end – it's not *in itself* their intended outcome. To understand the service-need, we must describe that outcome in *business* terms, usually distinct from the service itself. To use an example from the ITIL v3 specification, we ourselves might think of our service as delivering "an online sales-information process" or suchlike, but what our service-customer actually wants is something that will enable their salespeople to spend more time face to face with their own customers. *That's* the real need; *that's* what we need to design our service for; *that's* the real measure of "success" in service terms – a satisfied customer. How we get to that desired outcome is up to us: to a large extent, the client doesn't want to know, as long as the outcome *is* achieved.

This brings us back to those core principles of service-oriented architecture: loosely coupled, contract-based, discoverable, interchange, abstraction, and so on. Those support best-value for the customer. Other principles support best-value for *us* as service-providers: particularly reusability, composability, and, again, a layered abstraction. But these depend, in turn, on that fundamental shift in perspective: that *everything* in the enterprise is a service.

It's not an easy shift in perspective, perhaps, but the payoffs can be huge – especially in terms of simplicity, clarity, resilience, and speed of response to change. Yet to make it work well, we need another parallel shift in perspective, about the way we view the enterprise *as* a whole. And that shift is what we need to look at next.

# Into Practice

- What to you is "service-oriented architecture"? How would you apply such ideas in your existing enterprise?

- How do you address the security and identity-management issues in service-oriented architecture? And the synchronous-transaction issues?

- What structures and processes do you use for service-management? Do they only apply to IT-services or to other services as well?

- Who are the clients for your services? How do you identify and model their business needs and business outcomes? How do you ensure that your services deliver against those outcomes?

- What distinctions do you currently draw between products and services? Who are the users and "consumers" of each? In what ways do those users differ, in terms of expectations, responsibilities, and so on?

# Summary

In this chapter, we explored how, as with enterprise architecture, service-oriented architecture has often been associated almost exclusively with low-level IT. However, we *can* break free from that restriction, and open out to the whole scope of enterprise architecture, by recognizing that *everything* within the enterprise either is, provides, or represents a service.

In the next chapter, we'll review two core metaphors for the enterprise: the enterprise as a machine and as a living entity in its own right.

# CHAPTER 3

# Basics – A Matter of Metaphor

For at least a hundred years, the dominant metaphor of business has been that of "enterprise as a machine." The science behind its notion of "scientific management" is essentially Newtonian, a clockwork universe following implacable, supposedly universal "laws of business." And there's no doubt that it did work well, for the business-owners at least; Ford's assembly-lines were hailed as marvels of their age, as productivity leapt manyfold under the ever-vigilant eye of the time-and-motion man.

But times have moved on, and despite the evident desire of so many managers to cling on to the apparent certainties of the past, it's clear that the old-style "scientific management" has long passed its own "use-by" date. It's not wrong, as such, but in practice, it's a special case, one that only works well in stable markets with stable products and slow rates of change – a business context which these days has often become an almost unheard-of luxury. To cope with the complexities of the real business world of the present, we need an approach which is more flexible, more resilient, and much faster in response to change.

And if the times have moved on, so has the underlying science. A new version of Taylor's "scientific management" would have to include complexity-science, systems-theory, emergence, ecology, and living systems. To understand service-oriented architecture and the true nature of the service-oriented enterprise, a better metaphor is not "enterprise as

© Tom Graves 2023
T. Graves, *The Service-Oriented Enterprise*, https://doi.org/10.1007/978-1-4842-9189-4_3

a machine," but "enterprise as living organism." Yet the "machine" view is still so dominant in present-day business that it's worthwhile spending some time to explore the differences between these two core metaphors.

---

I perhaps need to emphasize at this point that all we're talking about here are metaphors as perspectives, different ways of looking at the business world. There's no politics here, no "should" or anything like that, no assertion that one is always "better" than the other. As I've said earlier, both metaphors do each have their valid uses in the right types of context. All we're exploring at this stage are the differences between the two metaphors and their implications in real-world practice; we'll see how to put the outcomes of this exploration into practice later on in the book.

---

## Structural Basis

In the machine metaphor, the enterprise is comprised of a myriad of small components. To work well, all of these components must mesh together, like gears inside a machine. Every part must be carefully designed, engineered, and machined to fit in its allotted place – in *only* that place – and must be interchangeable with any other part that matches the same specification. Every task has a predefined "job-description"; the machine has no real place for skill, and individual difference is almost anathema. Everything is a "resource," hence the term "human resources" – and hence too that bitter sense of feeling regarded as no more than "a cog in the machine" to be discarded on the scrap-heap as soon as our work is done.

In the organism metaphor, the enterprise is composed of a myriad of interdependent services, working together, as a community, toward a common purpose. Although there is some specialization – giving the appearance of radical difference in some cases – each of the cells ultimately shares the same underlying structure. The network of interdependencies is such that the overall structure, and even the set of cells within it, will automatically adapt itself to change and will spread the load in the event of damage. No part, however, is *directly* interchangeable with any other. Replacement will naturally occur, but the whole organism changes with each alteration, and what keeps the organism together under such change is that unifying purpose.

# Location of Purpose

In the machine metaphor, the key point is that the machine has no inherent or intrinsic purpose: it's just a machine. Any purpose for the machine has to come from *outside* of the machine itself. In the classic Victorian model, the machine – and hence everything and everyone in it – exists to serve the purpose of whoever is declared to be its "owner": the shareholders, in the present-day version of that model. In the commercial context, its purpose is as a "machine for making money." The means and mechanisms by which it does so are apparently almost irrelevant, as long as it does so to the owners' satisfaction; if not, the machine itself may be discarded, at whim.

---

In essence, this is the view mandated by much of present-day business-legislation, perhaps particularly in the United States, but also often in other countries.

---

In the organism metaphor, a *shared purpose* is fundamental to the existence of the organism. A purpose is *intrinsic*, not extrinsic: it comes from within the enterprise, not from outside. Means and mechanisms all need to align with that purpose in order to work well, and in essence, the organism owns itself.

One of the practical difficulties of the organism metaphor in a present-day commercial context is that it *doesn't* align well with the "shareholder-as-owner" model. As business commentator Charles Handy put it, "Companies today are quintessentially collections of people adding value to material things. It is not appropriate to 'own' collections of people. Particularly it is inappropriate for anonymous outsiders to own these far from anonymous people."

In short, the organism metaphor exposes the bleak fact that the current shareholder model asserts purported "ownership rights" that, in human terms, are dangerously close to slavery – which is *not* a stable or sustainable basis for any economy…

# Structure of Management

In the machine metaphor, management is a "thing apart": it exists to control the machine, on behalf of the "owners," but is separate and distinct from both. There's an almost absolute split between the "brain" and "brawn," often seen as a clash of opposites – management *vs.* workers, white-collar *vs.* blue-collar. Knowledge is deemed to reside *only* in management; the machine itself is presumed to be brainless – a "mere machine" – hence, all of its necessary thinking must be done by "outsiders" relative to the machine itself. And control of the implementation of that "external" thinking is distributed throughout the machine via a hierarchy of authority: the classic-management textbook distinctions between "staff" and "line."

In the organism metaphor, management is simply another service: it's intrinsic to every part of the enterprise. There's no inherent separation between the "brain" and "brawn" – indeed, the organism would fail if its brain were to be excised in the same way as in the machine-metaphor.

Knowledge and the ability to garner and apply that knowledge are all likewise distributed throughout the organism, with an emphasis on local knowledge applied to the local context. Management exists to support and guide, but does not attempt to control.

---

Most modern models for quality-management take this approach; for example, one of the core principles is that the knowledge to solve a problem in manufacturing is most likely to come from those who are closest to the work.

The catch is that this is almost the exact opposite view to the "machine-metaphor" management-knows-best model that still seems to be preferred in most management-education. But W Edwards Deming, one of the figureheads of the quality movement, was insistent on this point: most of the problems in quality had their roots in the structural failings of the management system, he said, and managers should look to their own behaviors first before blaming front-line workers for poor quality. Although he doesn't describe it in such terms, Deming's work provides one of the best descriptions of how the "living organism" metaphor applies in real practice, especially in the manufacturing context.

---

# Emphasis for Overall Improvement

In the machine metaphor, the main interests in improvement are about efficiency and reliability. Efficiency is seen as "doing more with less" – which in a business context usually means cutting costs, and cutting costs, and cutting costs yet again, in a relentless quest for the nirvana of getting everything for nothing. Reliability is supposedly important too, though in practice it often comes a distant second in priority to an imagined "efficiency."

In the organism metaphor, efficiency and reliability are recognized as just two out of five key factors in *effectiveness* – "efficient on purpose":

- *Efficient*: Makes the best use of the available resources

- *Reliable*: Can be relied on to deliver the required results

- *Elegant*: Supports the human factors in the context

- *Appropriate*: Supports and sustains the overall purpose

- *Integrated*: Linked to and supports integration of the whole *as* a whole

In the "living enterprise," performance depends on how well we *optimize* all the trade-offs across these dimensions that, together, express the enterprise's "ability to do work." Efficiency is neither the same as effectiveness nor separate from it, but is a *subset* of what's needed for overall effectiveness. Hence, improvements focus on the *balance* between these dimensions – not solely on a single theme such as efficiency.

---

These themes of enterprise effectiveness are explored in more depth in two other related books: *Real Enterprise Architecture: Beyond IT to the Whole Enterprise* and *SEMPER and SCORE: Enhancing Enterprise Effectiveness*. For more details, see Appendix B, "Resources."

---

# Resilience and Change

In the machine metaphor, there can be no inherent resilience as such: the enterprise is just a machine, with very limited options to adapt itself to change. The purpose, the brain, and even most of the senses are all "external": adaptation for change can only come from outside – hence the armies of self-styled "management consultants." The process of change is typified by such mechanistic terms as "restructuring," "business process reengineering," or John Zachman's notion of "engineering the enterprise." Everything in the machine is an interchangeable component, so a typical change-process will consist of pulling the machine apart, and then reassembling the components in a different order, according to some revised "system design." There is no real concept of human impact in any of this, because there's no real concept of people *as* people: they're "human resources," no different from any other enterprise asset. The only obvious difficulty – from within that metaphor, at least – is that response to change is usually reactive and slow; the result is that there's an apparently limitless need to keep tinkering with the machine, always running to keep up with an ever-changing reality, a futile search for the final, certain, stable "future state."

In the organism metaphor, the mesh of interdependencies provides the enterprise with inherent resilience to sway with the winds of change. The notion of *viable services* – which we'll explore further throughout this book – means that the enterprise becomes *self*-adapting, guided overall by the defined business purpose; the whole focus is "efficient *on purpose.*" The one serious difficulty posed by all that interdependence is that we can't pull the enterprise apart, in the same brutal way that we can in the machine-metaphor, and expect it to survive the change unscathed. If we truly do have to excise some part of the organism, we have to do so with a great deal of care.

---

Mergers can be difficult enough for a large enterprise, but demergers are often worse. Following the same enterprise-as-organism metaphor, we could suggest that survivability of such a split could depend on the complexity of the "organism": amoebas split themselves apart as an everyday activity, but humans don't!

In some cases, there might be a useful analogy here with lizards that can regrow a tail; or with the axolotl, which can even regrow an entire missing limb; or also with so-called "superorganisms" such as a beehive or an ant-nest, in which the "organism" is itself composed of near-autonomous, semi-independent individuals.

Yet the oddest and certainly most interesting analogy would be with the unfortunately named slime-molds. They start out as individuals barely bigger than an amoeba, but can merge together into a strange anarchic entity, a kind of gigantic single-cell creature, in some species up to a meter or more across, with many independent nuclei moving around inside it – metaphorically speaking, an enormous enterprise with a completely "flat" management-structure. They have some similarities to fungi, but as a collective entity can move around in search of food, at speeds of almost a meter a minute – far faster than any individual cell. And when food runs out completely – or, metaphorically, when the collective enterprise finally fails – the whole thing splits apart again back into individual cells, which waft away into the breeze as microscopic spores, to start the cycle all over again. The ultimate demerger, perhaps...

But the point here is that when we view the enterprise as an organism, we recognize that whatever we do to change the enterprise, we can't just wrench it all apart without doing some serious damage; it has to be done with a great deal more subtlety and care than in the machine-metaphor's "reengineering."

# Services in the Living Enterprise

In the machine-metaphor, we would typically describe units of the enterprise in terms of mechanistic *components*, linked together into larger and larger assemblies. But in the organism metaphor, the natural descriptors are cells and *services*: layer upon layer of them, interacting, interweaving, interdependent services, each delivering something of vital service and value to the overall enterprise.

The machine-metaphor for the enterprise isn't wrong as such; it's just that it's often too limited for what we really need, in order to understand the enterprise *as* an enterprise, and how to work with it in an architectural sense. The machine-metaphor's components describe the *composition* of the enterprise; the organism-metaphor's services describe what it *does*, and *is* and who and how it serves.

As per that previous definition, an enterprise is a community of some kind, coordinating its actions and resources in support of some shared mission and purpose. And that purpose – "that which it serves" – must always be greater than itself. Each service has an identifiable customer, with whom it shares a common "higher purpose" – hence the need for the purpose to have an enterprise-scope that is broader than that of the organization alone. As we move up the layers of services to reach the scope of "the enterprise as a whole," we gain a broader yet more precise view of the ultimate "higher purpose" for the enterprise.

---

Before we risk wandering off into the realms of religion and the rest, remember that all of this is still only a metaphor! Think of these descriptions as an "*as-if*," not an "*is*": it's just an analogy, not the thing itself.

The point is that both the organization and the customers for its services – whatever they may be – need some kind of shared "higher purpose" in order to bond together *as* an enterprise for that exchange of services. The classic way to describe this is in terms of vision, role, mission, and goal: the enterprise *vision* describes that common "higher purpose," the *role* describes how the enterprise sees itself in relation to that purpose – in other words, the services it provides for that purpose – while the *mission* is the enterprise capabilities that underpin that role, and so on. We won't be covering much more about that particular layering here, but there's more detail on the "visioning" process in the "Architecture on Purpose" chapter in the book *Real Enterprise Architecture* – see Appendix B, "Resources," for more details on that.

---

A simple organism is self-contained: it's *viable* within itself, but doesn't interact that much with other organisms – it doesn't offer or consume many services – and probably doesn't have much of a purpose, either. But even in a basic bacillus, there's some specialization within the structure, and this specialization is replicated on larger and larger scales as we move upward in levels of organic complexity, with individual cells, then clusters of cells, then entire organs, providing the myriad of specialized services that the overall organism – or enterprise – will need.

To make sense of how this works in the *viable enterprise*, we need some kind of overview or conceptual structure. So that's what we'll look at next, before going on to apply those principles in business practice.

# Into Practice

- In what ways do you describe the enterprise, or aspects of the enterprise, as parts of a machine? How is this reflected in the everyday language of the enterprise, such as "operations," "functions," "business units," and the like?

- In what ways do you describe the enterprise, or aspects of the enterprise, as being some kind of living organism? How is this reflected in the everyday language of the enterprise, such as "culture," "health," "taking the pulse," or even the term "corporation" itself as a literal "embodiment"?

- What other metaphors do you use to describe the enterprise? How are these reflected in the everyday language of the enterprise, such as "getting a green light" (a "roads" metaphor), "taking a bet" (a metaphor of finance as gambling), or "cooking up a new project," perhaps?

- What impact do such metaphors have on the operation and existence of your enterprise? In the short term? Medium term? Long term?

# Summary

In this chapter, we found that the most common metaphor for the enterprise is to view it as some kind of complicated yet controllable machine. But to succeed with a whole-of-enterprise architecture that is based on services, we have to shift our perspective and view the enterprise more as a kind of living organism in its own right, with its own self-chosen direction and purpose.

In the next part of this book, we'll start to explore the principles and structures that underpin the service-oriented enterprise.

# PART II

# Principles – An Overview

The core principles of service-oriented architecture and design are well-documented from the work on IT-services:

- Encapsulation of subcomponents into bundles of more usable functionality

- Loose-coupling via messages and standards

- Service-contracts between "requester" and "provider" roles

- "Black-box" abstraction of the internal workings of services

- Design for reuse and repurpose

- Self-advertising of capabilities and interface needs to enable "discoverability"

As we move beyond detail-level IT, though, other concerns may also come into play. One is that there may need to be multiple implementations of a service, to allow for operational issues such as upscaling, downscaling, and disaster-recovery. Another is that we need to be aware of the different types of services and how they interrelate with each other – see Chapter 4, "Principles – The Structure of Services." And we also need to be clear about the distinctions between the service-types themselves:

- Services that provide the *deliverables* of the enterprise, or directly support those deliverables – see Chapter 5, "Principles – Delivery Services"

- Services that *manage* the enterprise and its services – see Chapter 6, "Principles – Management Services"

- Services that provide the *coordination* for end-to-end processes – see Chapter 7, "Principles – Coordination Services"

- Services that promote, protect, and preserve the *pervasive values* of the enterprise – see Chapter 8, "Principles – Pervasive Services"

We need to remember, too, that none of these services exists in isolation: every service has its own set of relationships and interdependencies, all interweaving through the "value-web" that is the whole enterprise. To make sense of all of this from an architectural perspective, we need some means to clarify the complexity. The best way to do this is to describe the interactions in terms of architectural patterns, typically derived from formal systems-theory – see Chapter 9, "Principles – Properties and Patterns."

# CHAPTER 4

# Principles – The Structure of Services

Architecture is in part about structure and about the way that the various components fit together within that structure; so it's easy to see how most current styles of enterprise-architecture would naturally align themselves with a machine-metaphor for the enterprise. In that sense, the nature of architecture itself is part of the problem here.

Yet living entities have their structure too – though we do need to remember that it *is* a living entity, not a dead machine! So to extend that metaphor a little further, what is the anatomy of a service? Or its physiology?

Perhaps the simplest place to start is the machine-metaphor's split between the "brain" and "brawn." Even the simplest bacillus will show some internal specialization, and by the time we get to a true stand-alone cell such as an amoeba, there's some definite structure there. In particular, there's a single distinct nucleus somewhere near the center, which acts much like the entity's "brain," and a variety of smaller structures such as mitochondria, lysosomes, and vacuoles scattered throughout the cytoplasm that provide various support-functions and act as the cell's "brawn."

© Tom Graves 2023
T. Graves, *The Service-Oriented Enterprise*, https://doi.org/10.1007/978-1-4842-9189-4_4

The cell itself exists within a broader environment, in which it will serve some purpose, in an ecological sense at least. So in the abstract, hierarchical terms typified by classic "scientific management," we could summarize this visually as shown in Figure 4-1.

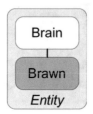

*Figure 4-1.* *"Brain" and "brawn"*

Extending the "scientific management" view further into the business context, the cell-like service exists to serve the purpose set by the external "owners," as shown in Figure 4-2.

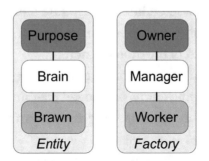

*Figure 4-2.* *Machine-metaphor model of a service*

In anything larger than the most minimal organism, the cell exists within a hierarchy of larger cell-like structures that replicate on larger scales the specializations that exist within each individual cell. So too in the enterprise: services are aggregated into larger-scale services, each encapsulating some specific functionality for the enterprise. Each service has its own "customers" and its own role within the overall purpose, and the same is true for every subservice and sub-subservice and so on.

Yet the layering of services is such that the "brain/brawn" pair of a single service becomes part of the "brawn" for the next layer upward in the hierarchy. So here we meet one of the fundamental flaws in "scientific management": it asserts an absolute split between white-collar and blue-collar, "brain" and "brawn," but in functional terms, *"brain" and "brawn" together form a single, indivisible unit.* The "brain" cannot be regarded as something separate, but in effect is distributed throughout the entire enterprise, *interwoven* with its "brawn." If we try to treat them as separate, we break down that "interwovenness"; the service then ceases to be viable – and with it, perhaps, the overall enterprise.

---

By the nature of cell-anatomy, the machine-metaphor's separation of the "brain" and "brawn" does sort of work at the lowest "cell-like" levels of the enterprise, and perhaps gives a pleasing illusion of control at the highest levels. Yet the metaphor's insistence on treating all "brawn" as brainless – and the "brain" likewise as "brawnless" – will guarantee intractable problems anywhere in the middle and ultimately renders the entire enterprise unworkable, as we can see all too easily in practice – but perhaps not so easily see *why*…

---

Looking at a single cell in a microscope, it's quite easy to identify the nucleus and the other individual subservices. But it can be easy to forget that all of these subentities are enclosed within the one cell-wall and operate *as* a *single unit* and also easy to forget that each cell will usually be part of a larger structure, which itself will be part of a larger structure, and so on. And it's also easy to become distracted by the fact that within each cell, there will be many subsidiary services, and often many instances of a particular type of subsidiary service, yet just *one* nucleus, one "brain."

There are a few rare examples, such as the slime-molds mentioned earlier, in which there may be multiple nuclei within the one overall cell, but we can probably leave those out of this discussion for now. In a sense, though, this *does* apply to the organization as comprised of a collective of living people, each with their own brain and more, with all of the variability and complexity that this implies. Something worth thinking about, perhaps?

Given that apparent uniqueness, it's easy to see how management – the business equivalent of the cell's nucleus – would tend to think of itself as "special and different." That delusion does even sort of make sense at the highest levels of the enterprise, and at the very lowest, because in both cases there's just the one nucleus on the chart – at the top, nothing below than brawn; at the bottom, nothing above but management. But in the middle, as shown in Figure 4-3, the delusion falls apart: up, down, sideways, there has to be both "brain" *and* "brawn." There, management is not and cannot be "special and different": it's just one more service among many, and nothing more than that.

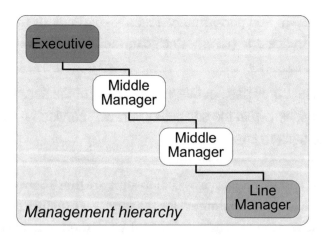

***Figure 4-3.*** *Breakdown of "special and different" delusion in the middle layers*

Something else that's easy to miss in the microscope – in fact, very hard to see – is the process of communication and coordination that occurs both between the subsidiary services within the cell and between the cell and other cells with which it's associated. To make sense of viable systems, we need to understand not just the visible services but also the more subtle web of connections between them.

# Service Relationships

At this point, we can drop the cell-analogy, and go straight to business. What we're mainly interested in here are the differences between *intraservice* relationships – those that occur within the service itself – and *interservice* relationships that link between services, vertically, horizontally, and in other ways.

The main intraservice relationships are those between the "brain" and "brawn" – the subsidiary *delivery-services* that do the concrete work of the overall service unit. In classic business terms, there are requirements and definitions of "critical success factors" (CSFs) going downward from "brain" to "brawn" and performance-records – particularly the "key performance indicators" (KPIs) – that go upward from "brawn" to "brain."

---

More precisely, they pass between the "brain" of the service and the "brain" services *within* the subsidiary "brawn" services – a point we'll come back to later.

---

The most visible interservice relationships are those between the overall service and the "customer" for the service – usually called the "requester" in service-oriented architecture. The requirements for these relationships are typically documented in some form of service-level agreement (SLA) or operational-level agreement (OLA), which should – but sometimes doesn't – also define the metrics by which the quality of service would be monitored. So if we view a typical business-function as a service, we would expect to see a structure something like that shown in Figure 4-4.

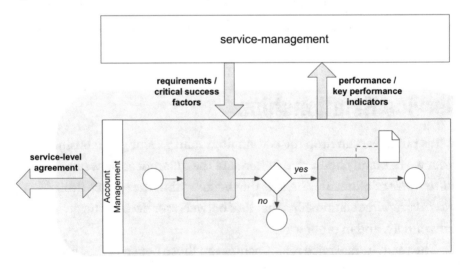

***Figure 4-4.*** *A simple example of business function as encapsulated service*

That's probably all of the relationships that would be described in a typical IT-centric version of service-oriented architecture. In fact, in most cases, we'd be lucky to be presented with anything more than the basic "brawn to brawn" service-to-service transactions, without any quality-of-service metrics at all – which is a serious problem in itself for IT service-management.

But in addition to those missing metrics, there are also further key interservice relationships of which we need to keep track. Although there are others, as we'll see later, the most obvious of these are the extensions of the same intraservice relationships – requirements, CSFs, KPIs, and so on – up and down the service-hierarchy tree, as shown in Figure 4-5. Requirements cascade downward; report-metrics cascade upward, as described in Balanced Scorecard and the like.

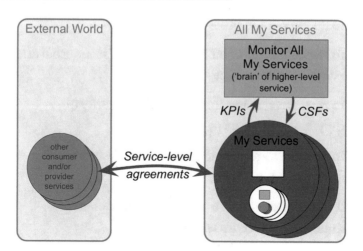

***Figure 4-5.*** *Hierarchy of services, each with their own performance-measures*

Each "brawn" within the service is really a complete service in its own right, so to some extent those "intraservice" relationships and messages are actually *inter*service relationships between the "brain" of the "parent"-service and the "brain" of the respective "child"-service. *The "brain" of* *the service is itself a service*: in most cases, its main "customers" are other "brain" services upstream and downstream in the service-hierarchy.

In addition to these, there are also a variety of "horizontal" relationships that focus not just on individual transactions but coordination of the full end-to-end processes in which the service takes part. And when we remember that in a real enterprise this will include *human* contexts as well as the machine-to-machine messages, we also need to include some other, often more subtle relationships and "transactions" around auditing, monitoring, quality, and trust that keep each service and the overall enterprise on track and "on purpose."

When we look at all the requirements of an enterprise, viewed in terms of the living-organism metaphor, we can see that *every* subunit in the enterprise would need to have some means to do all of the following:

- To *do* its task – in other words, deliver its services

- To *sense* and report on its perception of its internal and external environment

- To *remember*, using some kind of repository of knowledge about its past

- To *coordinate* its activities with other systems and services

- To *plan* its activities in some way, coordinating strategies and tactics with others

- To *adapt* to and, where possible, improve its own environment and operation

- To maintain a sense of *purpose*, to contrast its present condition with a desired future condition

Every living system does all of this in some way: even an amoeba has a sense of purpose and direction, if only in terms of a simple reflex response to its chemical context. Every part of a functioning enterprise does all of this, too – because if it doesn't, or if it doesn't do it well, the enterprise won't survive. This means that if we want to build a true architecture of the service-oriented enterprise, this is the true scope that we have to be able to describe, and to model.

But if this all seems a lot to include in a service-oriented architecture, don't worry. The principles, and even the practice, have all been well-documented for decades, in the formal discipline of management cybernetics, "the science of effective organization." And for this we can turn to *the* fundamental tool in that field: Stafford Beer's "Viable System Model."

# Services As Viable Systems

A *viable system* is any organized system that combines, and resolves to its benefit, all of the "survival demands" in a changing environment. In business terms, that means an enterprise that not only survives change but *thrives* on it, and for a service-oriented architecture, that implies a structure that is not only capable of monitoring its environment, and any changes in that environment, but also *self*-adapting to change wherever practicable.

So the Viable System Model (VSM) describes the fundamental structure and organization of any viable system. In essence, it's a service-oriented architecture, in much the same sense as in the previous section.

---

We won't need to go into the full detail of the VSM here – for that, see Stafford Beer's book *Brain of the Firm* or Patrick Hoverstadt's excellent *The Fractal Organization*. One of the model's most important characteristics, though, is its recursive structure: the same basic pattern repeats at every level of the enterprise. As a result, it has extraordinary *scalability*: it has been used for every type and size of organization, from small cooperatives in Britain, and mid-sized factories in Spain, all the way up to the management of the entire economy of a country – Allende's Chile, way back in the early 1970s.

Beer's "Cybersyn" system for Allende not only created a true "balanced scorecard" technique two decades before Balanced Scorecard but also showed how to use that information to make real-time decisions about the operations of a huge enterprise. The system worked well until it was destroyed during a military coup. Sadly, the Chilean website that used to describe the project in detail no longer seems to exist, but even the Wikipedia page about it – see Appendix B, "Resources" – is a real eye-opener about what can be achieved when even very limited resources are combined with a few truly innovative ideas. Many of those ideas will still seem advanced even by today's standards, several decades later. Go see for yourself: *very* strongly recommended for any enterprise architect or IT-architect.

---

The VSM was originally intended as a way to describe the actions and information-flows needed for management of the system – the metaphoric equivalent of a nervous-system for the "viable enterprise," but not much more than that. So while it's a powerful model from an IT-architecture perspective, it does need some expansion to make it work well as a generic model for *all* types of "viable services," rather than solely for "viable IT-systems." We'll explore that later; for now, the main point is that it starts from the same basic "brain/brawn" split that we've seen earlier as a base to understand the structure of services.

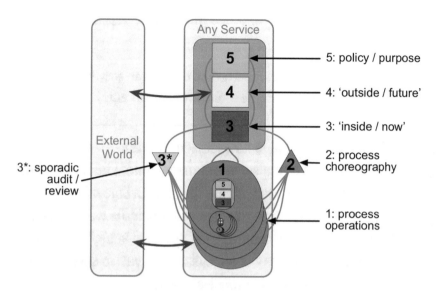

***Figure 4-6.*** *Specialized subsystems with each service in the Viable System Model*

In the model summarized in Figure 4-6, Beer represents these by a rectangle for the "brain" – the management-services – and a circle for the "brawn," the delivery-services. Each "brain" can manage any number of "brawn" units – each of which in turn contains its own "brain" and any number of subsidiary "brawns." Crucially, Beer splits the "brain" into three distinct subsidiary functions and includes two other functions which are, in part at least, *outside* of the "brain/brawn" pair.

In the VSM, all of these functions or "systems" are assigned numbers, as follows:

- *system-5*: Maintain the *policy*, purpose, and identity

- *system-4*: *Research* and report on the external environment, and develop a *strategy*

- *system-3*: *Plan* and *manage* the operations activities

- *system-3\**: *Monitor* and *verify* by sporadic audit of activities

- *system-2*: *Regulate* and *coordinate* activities with other systems and services at a tactical level

- *system-1*: *Do* the allotted task of the overall service, and sense and report on the internal environment

---

In the original model, what is now labeled "system-3*" was first considered to be part of the system-3 management tasks. Practical experience, though, such as with the Chilean "Cybersyn" project, showed that it did need to be handled separately. As we'll see later, the VSM assignment for system-3*, as "sporadic audit," is actually only one of a whole category of subsidiary "pervasive services" with this relationship to the management-services.

---

A glance back at that list at the end of the previous section would show that these VSM "systems" cover most of those requirements: the only items missing are the two about knowledge and memory, and adaptation and improvement. Although both of those are partly covered by the definition for system-4, they're actually better handled by an expansion of the roles of system-2 and system-3*, as we'll explore in more depth later on in the book.

Although the VSM itself focuses on management (the system-3, system-4, system-5 cluster) and the information-flows needed for management, the real tension of importance in the enterprise is between the purpose (the single top-level system-5) and the expression of that purpose in practice (the multitude of system-1 entities). *Everything else – including management – is just a support-service toward that end.*

Without those support-services, the purpose won't happen; hence, management does matter, and matter a lot. But we do need to keep a perspective here, and perhaps a better perspective even than the VSM itself: we need to give equal attention to *all* of the services and service-categories, at every level and of every type, and avoid any overemphasis on just one or two at the expense of all the others.

In effect, every service, whatever its level in the service-hierarchy, has the same internal structure and relationships; yet each has its own specialist role within the organism or, at a broader whole-of-enterprise scale, the superorganism. Each service has its own set of subsidiary services or "child-services" with four possible categories of functions:

- *Task-delivery or delivery-support (system-1)*: See Chapter 5, "Principles – Delivery Services."

- *Service-management (system-3, system-4, system-5)*: See Chapter 6, "Principles – Management Services."

- *"Horizontal" coordination with other services (system-2)*: See Chapter 7, "Principles – Coordination Services."

- *Functions to keep the overall service on track and aligned with enterprise purpose (system-3\*)*: See Chapter 8, "Principles – Pervasive Services."

Classic management texts would bundle everything other than task-delivery into the service-management services. But as the VSM diagram shows, coordination and audit *do* need to be addressed separately – not least because they need to operate under a different type of management-structure, and operate in a completely different way to the vertical hierarchy of the main service-management.

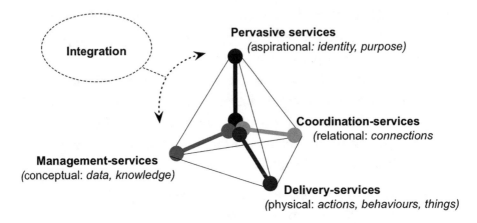

***Figure 4-7.*** *Service-functions and the tetradian architecture-dimensions*

As shown in Figure 4-7, the four types of services also align with the four architecture-dimensions of the *tetradian* model:

- *Delivery services*: *Physical* dimension – actions and transactions

- *Management services*: *Conceptual* dimension – information, planning, and reporting

- *Coordination services*: *Relational* dimension – connections between people and across the silos

- *Pervasive services*: *Aspirational* dimension – enterprise purpose, identity, and values

We also need to explore how the different types of services communicate with each other – see Chapter 9, "Principles – Properties and Patterns." In most cases, these would pass through predefined "normal channels" – though note that many of these, particularly with people-based services, could use a range of means that may be much broader than just the usual IT-type transactions, records, and messages. But in some cases, an emergency-message or other exceptions – what Beer describes as an "algedonic" or literally "pain/pleasure" communication – may need to jump from *any* service to any other, and these must be able to bypass those "normal channels" completely, whether middle-management likes it or not! So while the VSM does describe all the information-channels needed by a complete viable-system, it's not always either the same or as simple as conventional IT-centric descriptions might expect.

For now, though, let's look at each of those service-function types in more detail – starting with the main task-delivery functions.

# Into Practice

- What structures of services would you identify in your existing enterprise? In what ways are these services layered, repeating the same kind of structure at different hierarchical levels?

- In what ways are these services and their structures divided between the "brain" and "brawn"? Who or what sets the overall purpose for each structure?

- In what ways do these services communicate with each other? Via what mechanisms? And for what purposes?

- How are the activities of the various services coordinated? At each level? Between levels? And as nodes within end-to-end processes?

- How would you identify the efficiency, reliability, and overall effectiveness of any service? Or of communication and coordination within and between services? How would you improve any of this? What support – or lack of it – do you gain from the service's structure itself in doing so?

# Summary

In this chapter, we started from the machine-metaphor notion of a strict separation between management and workforce, the "brain" and "brawn," and its implications in relation to services. From there, we explored Stafford Beer's "Viable System Model" as a basic structure to describe services and their interrelationships within any layer of the enterprise.

In the next chapter, we'll look at the first set of services in the Viable System Model, the "delivery services" that deliver value to the enterprise.

# CHAPTER 5

# Principles – Delivery Services

In the service-oriented enterprise, service-delivery is what the enterprise *does*. Exactly what it delivers, and how it does so, will depend on the nature of the enterprise and on the layer of detail in scope, but it's always about some kind of action or transaction, something that is done.

Technically speaking, every service is a "delivery service," since by definition every service delivers something for some specified "customer." What we're talking about in this section, though, are those services that deliver something of value to the enterprise's external customers, either directly or in direct support of that external-service delivery.

Remember too that every service actually has the same structure; *every* service delivers something, manages itself, coordinates itself with others, and aligns to the overall values of the enterprise. In these sections, we'll explore the effective emphases of each type of service – the roles they play within the enterprise and its purpose – but in terms of their *internal* structure, they're all much the same. The specific implementations of each service may differ a lot, of course, but that's something else we'll look at later.

The bulk of the enterprise is made up of delivery-services, in an often-bewildering variety of forms and at a multitude of levels of detail and abstraction. A service may also be delivered by *any* appropriate combination of people, machines, and IT, though with the emphasis here on "fitness for purpose" rather than on the means of implementation – a key point that IT-architects do sometimes tend to forget!

Delivery-services will typically be split into three categories:

- *External-delivery* to an end-customer or other service-consumers elsewhere in the enterprise

- *Internal-delivery*, where the "customer" is another service within the enterprise, and what is delivered is "core" to the enterprise purpose

- *Infrastructure* and other support-services that are "noncore" to the enterprise purpose

There are no intrinsic distinctions between these categories, no *inherent* reason why any given type of service should always be placed in one category than another: the distinctions depend on context, not content. Building-maintenance or cleaning-services, for example, might be regarded as "noncore" infrastructure by most organizations, but would be the "core" external-delivery for a company that provided glazing services or cleaning-materials. So although – like the various organs in the human body – they may take different forms and have different functions in the enterprise, these are *all* "delivery-services" and structurally should be treated in exactly the same way.

# Viable System Context

In viable-system terms, these are the *VSM system-1* services.

In VSM diagrams, as shown in Figure 5-1, these are represented by a circle, which also contains within itself the nested sets and subsets of its "child" VSM systems.

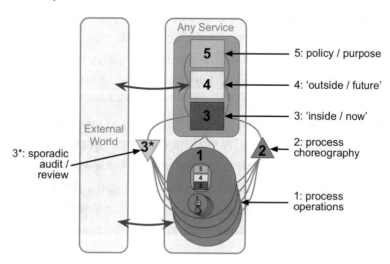

**Figure 5-1.** *VSM "systems"*

In the tetradian architecture-model, these typically represent the *physical* dimension.

In the organism-metaphor, these might represent, for example, the muscles, tendons, and sinews ("external delivery"), digestion and lungs ("internal delivery"), and vascular systems and skeleton ("infrastructure") of the enterprise. These also provide the real-world sensors that deliver sense-information for all subsequent decision-making.

# Enterprise Context

At the most abstract level of the enterprise – as shown by system-1 entities in the top-level VSM diagram in Figure 5-1 – there would be at least one delivery-service, up to perhaps a maximum of seven. (In practice, anything more than around seven is likely to become too unwieldy to manage.)

The number of top-level delivery-services is determined by the number of *distinct* customer-groups or markets that the enterprise will service – "distinct" in the sense of fundamentally different needs and services, rather than simple market-categories such as age-group or geographic distributions – plus an arbitrary set of high-level internal support-services.

At the board-level, these would typically be represented by the Chief Operations Officer (COO), and perhaps also by the Chief Technical Officer (CTO) in an IT-oriented enterprise. Given the prominence of finance in most organizations, those support-services would probably also be represented at the board-level by the Chief Finance Officer (CFO).

In the body of the enterprise, the delivery-services would be represented by explicit business-units and work-teams, often split on functional or geographic boundaries. The actual services would be delivered by any appropriate combination of people, machines, and IT.

# Subunits or Variants

From a VSM perspective, all delivery-services are equal: there are no subunits or variants as such. But as described earlier, there are in effect three subtypes – external-delivery, internal-delivery, and infrastructure – though the distinctions between them are often more about role and perception than any intrinsic difference. These distinctions would become more evident as we move downward into the following detail-hierarchy.

# External Delivery (Value Chain)

At the higher levels, the "external customer" for external-delivery services would literally be external, an "outside" stakeholder. At the detail-levels, it's more often that the service is directly in-line within a value-chain: there is an *end customer* for the overall value-chain, but the direct "customer" for the delivery-service will often be the next service in line in the end-to-end business-process.

Each service should usually have a single defined type of "customer" or service-consumer at the respective level of abstraction. Note, though, that the opposite is not necessarily true: that "customer" may itself consume services from any number of suppliers.

There are an infinite variety of forms of delivery-service and service-content, each dependent on the industry and context. A law-firm, for example, might deliver the following external services:

- Legal advice

- Court representation

- Contract preparation and review

- Conveyancing of commercial property

To the organization, its external-delivery services are invariably perceived as "core" business functions: without them, the reason for the enterprise in its present form would probably cease to exist. As a result, they are usually described as "profit-centers" in corporate accounts.

## Internal Delivery (Support Services)

The "customer" or service-consumer for an internal-delivery service is another service internal to the enterprise: it will not have any direct contact with an external customer of the enterprise.

Each internal-delivery service will typically have only a small number of "customer"-types at the respective level of abstraction – perhaps only one. It may itself be a customer of any number of suppliers.

Examples in the law-firm might include

- Library

- Physical-records archive

- Database, knowledge-base, and information-systems

Internal-delivery services are usually perceived as "core" business functions: in some cases, the enterprise could perhaps obtain them from other service-providers, but would not be able to do so with high efficiency or effectiveness. As a result, although they are usually described as "cost-centers" in corporate accounts, they are rarely available for outsourcing.

## Infrastructure Services

As for internal-delivery services, the "customer"-type for an infrastructure service is another service internal to the enterprise. It will usually not have any direct contact with an external customer of the enterprise. It may in reality exist only in virtual form within the enterprise, in that it is actually delivered by an external service-provider – a "supplier" to the enterprise.

Each infrastructure service will typically have many "customers" at the respective level of abstraction. It may itself be a customer of any number of suppliers.

Examples in the law-firm might include

- Energy and other consumables

- Building-management and maintenance

- Logistics and mail-services

- Provision of office-consumables

- Recruiting, salary, benefits, expenses, and other routine people-management

- Training and certification

Infrastructure services are usually perceived as "noncore" business functions: the enterprise could operate without them as internal services, or obtain them from other service-providers without significant detrimental impact on business efficiency or effectiveness. Often, such services, although essential, are regarded as a distraction from the main focus of the enterprise. As a result, they are usually described as "cost-centers" in corporate accounts, and are often available for outsourcing.

# Interfaces

Interfaces with service-customers (service as a ***provider***) and suppliers (service as a ***requester***) are all horizontal peer-to-peer relationships, at the same functional level (see Figure 5-2). Each of these interfaces would be defined and monitored through a service-level or operations-level agreement, which may be either explicit – such as in a contract, or a message-format – or implicit in a trust-relationship such as the stereotypic "gentlemen's agreement."

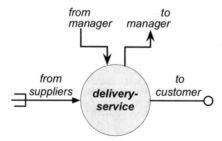

***Figure 5-2.***  *Delivery-service interfaces*

Secondary interfaces with other internal "systems" would include the following:

- *"Downward" from local management (system-3):* Schedules, priorities, and other requirements

- *"Upward" to local management (system-3):* Performance summaries, escalated exceptions

- *"Upward" to local strategy (system-4):* Future-context information gleaned from service-delivery activities

- *"Sideways" with local cross-silo coordination (system-2)*: Interservice schedules and other information-exchange for end-to-end processes

- *"Sideways" with any level of representatives for pervasive-services (system-3\*)*: Auditing, monitoring, and capability-development for alignment with enterprise values

Each delivery-service is an encapsulation of all of the subsidiary services needed to deliver the nominal service at that level of abstraction. Hence, there are many implied interfaces "downward" into the detail of the abstract service hierarchy, until eventually something real is delivered to a real customer or received from a real supplier.

---

There's a subtle point here that, for architects, is all too easy to miss: we're so used to working at an abstract level that it's easy to forget that the only *real* service is one right down at the root-level, at an actual "*touch-point*," that actually does something real, or exchanges something real with someone or something else. At every other level, it's just an abstract: for example, a customer-journey map or suchlike will help us understand what each service *would* be or do, or what it *would* or *should* receive or deliver, but it isn't real – it's still merely a model, nothing more than that. We'll often have to deliver reports about what it is that we're designing – but they're still only reports about something that still isn't yet real, and doesn't yet deliver anything real. Don't mix them up…

---

So note that unlike the management information-flows and suchlike, which often *are* reflected in tangible reports and other entities at each level of abstraction, *the root-level transactions are the only real items of service-delivery.* Every other nominal "service" above that root-level is an aggregation or abstraction for reporting purposes only, and does not exist as such in reality.

# Into Practice

- What services does your enterprise deliver as a whole? How would you identify and define the customers for those overall services?

- What distinctions and categorizations of customers start to appear as you move downward through the layers of abstraction, toward individual, explicit transactions?

- What are the "core services" of the enterprise? What services are "noncore"? By what means do you distinguish between "core" and "noncore"?

- If the corporate accounts use a categorization of "profit centers" vs. "cost centers," what characteristics are used to make such distinctions? What impact do such distinctions have on service-funding, on service-provision, on relationships between services, and on responsibilities for delivery or supply of those services?

- In what ways do you identify explicit delivery-services at each level of abstraction in the enterprise? How do the descriptions of "suppliers" and "customers" for these services change as you move downward toward the detail-layers of real service-delivery?

- Given a categorization of "external-delivery," "internal-delivery," and "infrastructure," how and why would you assign different delivery-services to each of those categories?

- What makes a service necessary to overall operation of the enterprise? What does each service deliver to the enterprise?

- What characteristics determine whether or not a given service is suitable for outsourcing, or purchase from an external service-provider?

## Summary

In this chapter, we reviewed the characteristics, roles, and interfaces for the "delivery" services of the enterprise. These provide what are most likely to be understood *as* the services of the enterprise – the visible work done by the organization's workforce and systems. In addition to those that deliver services or products to external customers, there are many that provide internal support in a multitudinous variety of forms. Some of these latter services may be outsourced – especially those "noncore" services that provide only a kind of background or infrastructural support.

In the next chapter, we'll explore the services that provide the various types of management-support for the enterprise.

# CHAPTER 6

# Principles – Management Services

In the service-oriented enterprise, management is about what the enterprise *knows*, how it *thinks*, and how it *decides*. Although the details will differ with each enterprise, there is actually very little difference in overall function or content or even in structure – hence one reason why managers may move from one enterprise to the next with relative ease, and relative success.

---

There's a subtle trap here that has killed many a company, and is very difficult to spot if you've been trained only in the Taylorist tradition of "scientific management." This is that while the management skills themselves may be portable, and the information-content for management is much the same everywhere, *that which is managed is not the same* – it's different with every context.

Taylorism assumes that the "brain" always knows best, and the higher up you are in the hierarchy, the more knowledge you're presumed to have. Hence, the "higher-ups" are assigned more authority, and more decision-making responsibility. So whenever there's a problem, or an exception to the predefined work-instructions in The Book, it's "escalated" upward in the hierarchy for decision, and "actions" passed back down again from on high as to what to do to resolve the problem.

But the catch is that this only works when the problem is one of conceptual knowledge. Often, the real need is not "thinking with the head" – the theory – but what we might call "thinking with the hands," which can only be gained through skills, through what may well be years of hard-won hands-on practical experience. Yet the Taylorist principles give preference and precedence to people who are strong on abstractions and strong on theory – but give little or no credit for competence in the practice. This means the "decision-makers" are less and less likely to be competent to make *practical* decisions – a situation that gets *worse* with each step higher up the tree, and often also over time as things change in their previous field of expertise.

As Deming demonstrated, the proper place for practical decisions is at the point of practice: sometimes, we need to "escalate" *down* in the hierarchy, not up. Yet in Taylorism, the workers at each level are deemed to be "brainless brawn" and have no power to make decisions. In effect, they have the nominal responsibility, but no authority. Instead, the authority is "owned" by the manager, and if the managers insist on holding on to responsibilities for detail-concerns for which they don't have the practical competence, *everyone* is stuck.

The only way to get "unstuck" is to ease off on the Taylorist top-down control, and instead to accept that "higher-up" knowledge is not necessarily "better" knowledge; rather, what matters is whether it's the *appropriate* knowledge. And the only way we can find out what type of knowledge *is* appropriate in any given context is by creating a respectful partnership of peers across the entire space. In that sense, management becomes "just another service," just like any other in the enterprise: theory serves practice just as much as practice serves theory.

I saw this approach used in real-world practice many times in my years as a systems-analyst in aircraft research. Each year, a new generation of bright young graduates would appear on the site, waving their shiny new engineering degrees, certain that they knew everything about aircraft design. And each year, with the full agreement of the foreman, and the senior management too, the machinists and fitters would smile, and go into a subtle work-to-rule: they would do *exactly* what the new engineers asked – which meant that nothing worked. Components were made for assemblies that couldn't be assembled; materials mated that wouldn't last more than a matter of minutes in the field; all precisely as per the design-specification... Some of the young engineers took longer than others, perhaps, but they all learned soon enough that there was another knowledge they needed here: a knowledge of how to make things work in the *real* world, rather than only the comfortable world of theory. If they wanted their designs to succeed in practice, they needed to respect that other knowledge, and work *with* it, no matter how different it was from their own.

---

Management-services form natural hierarchies, with each level representing a different layer of abstraction. Enterprise-architects would be familiar with some of these, such as from the classic Zachman set, with its five, six, or seven distinct layers, from unchanging "universals" at the top to the real-time maelstrom of operations at the bottom. Real enterprises will provide many variations on that theme, such as further splits on boundaries of geography or market or function, but the base-principle of a layered hierarchy of abstraction will remain the same.

Echoing the same layering, the Viable System Model embeds three distinct – and functionally different – layers within the "brain" of each system-1 delivery-service:

- *Policy*: Purpose, identity, imperatives, vision, and values

- *Strategy*: "Outside/future"

- *Direction*: "Inside/now"

The different functions of these subsystems also align to different abstractions of *time*, from far future all the way through to near past. Note, though, that these apply in their own ways within *every* system and service – not just at the top of the enterprise management hierarchy.

# Viable System Context

In viable system-terms, these are the **VSM system-3**, **system-4**, and **system-5** services.

In VSM diagrams, as shown in Figure 6-1, these are represented by a rectangle for the management-services collective set, containing three squares or rectangles for the three subsystems, with system-5 uppermost.

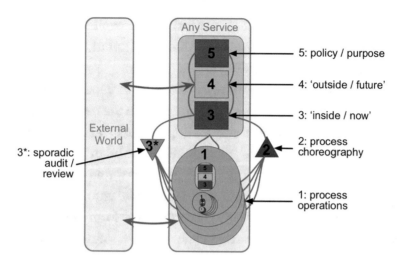

***Figure 6-1.*** *VSM "systems"*

In the tetradian architecture-model, these typically represent the *conceptual* dimension; system-5 also represents the management expression of the *aspirational* dimension.

In the organism-metaphor, these represent the brain and nervous-system of the enterprise – action-equests going out to the whole enterprise, and sense-information returning back, with decision-making taking place both centrally and distributed throughout the enterprise.

# Enterprise Context

At the most abstract level of the organization – as shown in Figure 6-1 by the bounding rectangle around the system-3, system-4, and system-5 entities in the top-level VSM diagram – there will be exactly one overall management service.

At the board-level, the system-5 ("policy") should be represented by the Chief Executive Officer (CEO) or Managing Director (MD). The system-4 ("strategy") would typically be represented by the whole board, with CEO or MD as chair, or perhaps ideally by an explicit role of Chief Strategy Officer (CSO). The system-3 ("direction") would typically be represented by the MD or COO.

In the body of the organization, the management-services would be represented by distinct groups or individuals with the respective assigned roles. For example, a formal strategy-group may take on responsibility for the system-4 "strategy" services directly below the board level; various staff-members will take on the system-3 "direction" role – often with a job-title of "manager" – at most levels within the organization. Further down in the hierarchy-tree, the respective tasks may well form only a part of the responsibilities of a work-role – especially for the system-4 "strategy" and system-5 "policy" tasks.

# Subunits or Variants

In the VSM, as described earlier, there are three distinct services that combine to make up the overall management-service within each system-1 unit: system-5 "policy," system-4 "strategy," and system-3 "direction."

---

While working on this chapter, I came across a point about the VSM that I hadn't noted before, and which may be important for anyone applying systems-theory principles in enterprise-architecture.

I base much of my own enterprise-architecture work on a rethink of Tuckman's well-known five-phase "Group Dynamics" project-life cycle, as an overview-model of the overall workings of an enterprise:

— *Forming*: Purpose, identity, strategy; also far-future

— *Storming*: People-issues; anywhere from far-future to far-past

— *Norming*: Plans and schedules; also near-future

– *Performing*: Production; also "*now*!"

– *Adjourning* (or *mourning*): Completions; also near-to mid-past

Yet when we look at the "management" section of the VSM, it seems it covers only three of the five Group Dynamics phases: VSM system-5 "policy" aligns to "forming"; system-4 "strategy" aligns to the later part of "forming," plus most of "norming"; and system-3 "direction" aligns to the later part of "norming," plus most of "performing."

But there's no explicit VSM coverage at all of the "storming" phase, the people-issues – which seems strange considering Beer's own strong personal bent toward people-oriented participatory politics. And although the original VSM "system-3*," "random-audit", does sort-of touch the "adjourning" phase, it only does so on an occasional basis – not the continuous processes needed for completions and lessons-learned.

This gap may stem from the VSM's history as a model of information-flows for management and the like, but it still seems a huge hole in the coverage of what's actually needed for systemic design of management processes. Odd…

We do cover these "missing" issues here, via our extended system-2 as "coordination services" and system-3* as "pervasive services." But if we use only the original VSM to describe management-services, we'll need some alternate means to cover those missing issues – or we'll once again end up with intractable issues that we can't see.

Management-services at any level should always include exactly one of each of these subsidiary services:

- Policy, purpose, and identity

- Strategy and situational-awareness (outward-facing)

- Direction and guidance (inward-facing)

We'll explore these in more detail in the following sections.

# Policy, Purpose, and Identity

The VSM system-5 "policy" service is responsible for "holding the vision" for the enterprise: anything to do with principles, policy, values, identity, and so on. Ultimately, it's also responsible for compliance to regulation and legislation, and defining how such should be interpreted in the enterprise – and that includes the more subtle "regulations" of the social milieu or corporate-culture in which the enterprise operates.

At the topmost level, the "policy" service sets the anchor – or perhaps "guiding star" – for the entire enterprise:

- **Purpose defines the enterprise priorities.**

Within each layer – each "system-1" instance – it's the role of the local "policy" service to interpret those priorities, and to assess and evaluate all activities in terms of those priorities. The function here is the enterprise's means to handle uncertainty: whenever we encounter a real-world context in which the usual rules don't apply, and analysis is either too misleading or too slow, the principles and purpose define the priorities to guide those decisions we need to make. Purpose *matters*.

But here we hit up against a nasty problem: there's almost always a difference between the principles and values that the enterprise would espouse in public, and the often-unconscious ones used in its actual decision-making. And sometimes that difference can be *huge* – so huge that no-one in the enterprise can see it (or, perhaps, take the risk of saying that they *do* see it...). Under those circumstances, what we'll need most is some perhaps painful-honesty, for which one useful guide is Stafford Beer's oft-quoted acronym POSIWID:

- **"The purpose of a system is what it does"**

If we don't like what the system does, or if what it's doing doesn't align to the espoused values, we need to look closer at how we're managing purpose in the enterprise. The *actual* "purpose" of the system is expressed in what it does – not just what we hope or believe or would like to pretend it does. If we say that safety is a high priority, yet we have a high accident-rate, what we've built is a system in which safety is actually a low priority: the problem is *systemic*, right at the core of the enterprise – and that misalignment is simply *reflected* in the work-practices, not caused by them.

To change that misalignment on safety – to use the same example – we would need to review *everything* in terms of safety: not just processes, but performance-metrics, work-incentives, knowledge-sharing, and the rest. So *the metrics we need to run the business are defined by the business-purpose*: the priorities define the content that we need in the enterprise "Balanced Scorecard."

---

Those metrics pass up and down the tree via the system-3 "direction" service – but to make sure that we can actually trust the figures and values reported in those metrics, and that they really do mean what they claim to mean, we need to verify that as well, by some kind of audit. We also need to support the root-level practices, and any changes needed in those practices, that end up being reported in those metrics. More on both of those concerns when we look later at the "pervasive services" – see Chapter 8, "Principles – Pervasive Services."

---

In the same way, purpose also acts as the guide and final arbiter for decision-making in strategy (VSM system-4), in direction (VSM system-3), and in the balance between them. As we move further down the tree, this "purpose" also includes constraints imposed by any applicable legislation and the like and also any standards either chosen by the enterprise or mandated or recommended by the market and milieu in which the enterprise operates – such as ISO-9000 certification for quality-systems-or an industry-specific XML-based messaging format. Purpose defines the standards, in every sense, by which the enterprise will measure itself – though this can get a lot harder to apply as the enterprise increases in size.

# Strategy and Situational Awareness ("Outside/ Future")

The VSM "system-4" service is responsible for assessing and interpreting the milieu and market in which the enterprise operates, to enable the enterprise to respond *proactively* to its environment. Typical themes include

- Scanning the business environment for context and for signs of future change

- Strategic foresight and forward planning, through tools such as scenario development and causal layered analysis

- Assessment of strategic risk

- Technical development, service development, product development, and capability development

Strategy is another whole field in itself – far more than we could cover here, given that the emphasis in this book is more on enterprise structure and architecture – so for now it's probably best just to leave it at that preceding summary. But there are plenty of good texts that do address those issues from an architecture-like perspective: see Appendix B, "Resources," for some examples.

Another key role of the "strategy" service is its engagement in "strategic conversations" between past and future for the enterprise: for example, sales (past) vs. marketing (future). Note, though, that this kind of "conversation" needs to occur at *every* level of the enterprise, as appropriate to the respective context – and not solely in a separate "strategy unit" that reports only to senior management.

## Direction and Guidance ("Inside/Now")

The VSM "system-3" service is responsible for coordination of all the activities in this service's "downstream" delivery-services – its collection of "system-1" instances. In short, this is the classic role of middle-management: a myriad of day-to-day decision and detail. This is the most visible aspect of the overall management services and usually accounts for the bulk of their work, too.

In poorly designed organizations, "direction" is often the only part of the management-services that exists lower down in the hierarchy-tree – which literally leaves the organization with only half a brain at those levels, capable only of dealing with the present and nothing else. *Not* a good idea…

In addition to directions to the "child" delivery-services, the two main tasks here are *resource management*, going downward, and *performance management*, coming back up the tree. Balancing the conflicts within and between these two tasks is rarely easy.

Resource-management sounds simple enough until we remember that those resources have to come from somewhere first, and then it's suddenly not so simple, particularly when large numbers of people are involved. As we'll see later in the discussion on coordination-services, there's another Taylorist trap that hits overly hierarchical organizations, because many of the resources have to come from *other* silos, and if we don't have good *horizontal* "silo-bridging" links, we'll be stuck with an unwieldy bureaucratic mess, which is no-one's idea of fun – and far from effective, too.

The other catch is that to know what resources we need for the "child" services, and how to divide the resources between them, we not only have to be clear about what we're asking them to deliver but also how we measure what they've delivered – in other words, the performance-metrics. If we get the design of the performance-metrics wrong, or if the goals aren't clear, or the metrics don't actually mean what they claim to mean, we'll again be stuck.

---

It gets even more complicated when – as is usually the case – there are delays in the system, because the performance measures will always be somewhat out of sync with the timing of the resource-allocation. By the time these constraints echo across even a simple supply-chain – such as the four-partner chain in the classic Beer Game simulation – it takes a great deal of skill, experience, *and mutual trust* to avoid an inefficient, ineffective, wasteful, frustrating, blame-filled mess. There are a fair number of online implementations of the Beer Game, so it's well worth having a go at it yourself: it's *not* easy.

The game was originally developed by Peter Senge and his colleagues at the Sloan School of Management, from the 1960s onward, as is explained in more detail in Senge's book on systems-theory, *The Fifth Discipline* – strongly recommended, anyway.

Yet another complication occurs with aggregation. In this section of the management-services, part of our task is to take all of the performance-metrics from the "child"-services, and aggregate them into a single set of metrics to pass upward in the tree. The catch here is that we need to ensure that the same definitions and transforms are used in each of the "children"; otherwise, we can no longer compare like with like, and the metrics risk being meaningless. The same applies further up the hierarchy-tree, particularly when we have to compare metrics from different silos. Once again, there's plenty of room for confusion here...

I came across a spectacular example of this in my work with a government department, when ministers and opposition almost came to blow over conflicting performance-figures that were supposedly derived from the same reporting-systems. They weren't the same systems, but the fact that all the files and data-fields had exactly the same names did kind of add to the confusion!

I've described this incident in other books, so I won't expand on it here; suffice it to say that this is where abstract-sounding notions such as "database of record" and "single source of truth" start to make real sense to the business-folks. More detail on this later when we look at "business systems" – see Chapter 12, "Practice – The Knowledge of Services."

And there is one more potential Taylorist trap of which we need to be aware: the tendency of managers to subsume all control of the coordination-services, and even the pervasive-services, into their own role. In part, this is because classic "scientific management" barely even acknowledges the need for such services; in part, this is because rigid-silo structures often lead to a desire to control and limit any "horizontal" connections, even though they're essential for any cross-silo end-to-end processes; and in part, it's because, if there's no explicit support or resourcing for such services, the "direction" management-service is probably the only place they can go, whether they fit there or not. But placing them there does cause all manner of intractable problems; more on those later in the respective sections in Chapter 7, "Principles – Coordination Services," and Chapter 8, "Principles – Pervasive Services."

# Overall Interaction

As shown in Figure 6-2, the overall management-service is delivered by the combined actions and interactions of the embedded system-3, system-4, and system-5.

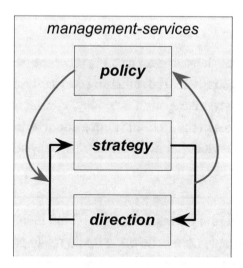

***Figure 6-2.*** *Management services: internal interactions*

System-3 "direction" and system-4 "strategy" need to engage in continual "strategic conversation" on a variety of themes such as

- Present sales vs. future marketing

- Present staff vs. future needs

- Present funding and resources vs. future needs

- Present products and production vs. future needs

System-5 "policy" acts as the arbiter in this conversation and also guides decision-making within each of the other two services. There would be some feedback into "policy" from both, but the main drivers to policy-change will tend to occur more from higher up in the hierarchy-tree.

# Interfaces

Management-services have symmetrical *vertical* connections, as both **provider** and **requester**, with the matching service-type above and below in the hierarchy-tree: system-5 "policy" connects to the "policy" management-services in the "parent" above and within the "child" system-1 delivery-services below, and likewise for system-4 "strategy" and system-3 "direction."

---

All of this might at first perhaps sound a bit too technical, "too much theory," but it actually comes down to some really practical questions: What information needs to flow up and down the management-hierarchy tree? How does policy link to strategy? How does strategy guide business-tactics? How will business-actics come into action at the line-management level? What connections do we need to make sure that all of those links work correctly, and the right information arrives in the right place at the right time? And how does all of this work together as a unified whole, even while the organization itself is undergoing all kinds of change all at the same time?

The whole purpose of the VSM here – and especially its view of management-services – is to provide us with a simple, consistent means to make sense of all of that complexity, which also works the same way everywhere, at every level of the management-tree.

---

At the top of the tree – in other words, the executive-management level – the "upward" connections link to the operating milieu and business-environment, the broader shared-enterprise. As shown in Figure 6-3, policy comes "down" in the form of legislation, regulation, standards, and social expectations; reporting goes "up," such as in the classic example of the company Annual Report.

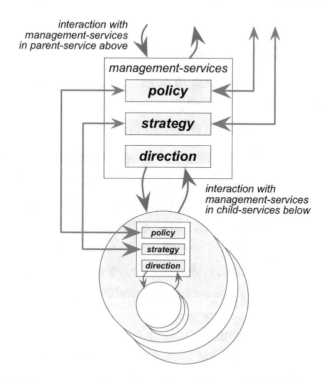

**Figure 6-3.** *Management services: interfaces with other systems*

Descending downward, the hierarchy-tree terminates wherever management finally connects with actual service-delivery. In those cases, "policy," "strategy," and "direction" do not connect with a matching counterpart, but with the service-delivery itself.

---

This is also the effective source of the key distinctions between "staff-management," "middle-management," and "line-management."

"Staff" are at the top of the hierarchy-tree: they connect to other management-services below, but must deal with the real-world business-milieu above.

Middle-managers are literally in the middle: they connect primarily with other managers both above and below.

Although line-managers report to other managers upward, they connect with *service-delivery* below – the horizontal links through which the "real-world" work actually happens.

So there's a subtle danger here that middle-managers need never see anything other than the abstract, vertically oriented world of management-services – an unfortunate trait whose disastrous consequences can be seen all too clearly in many organizations…

Because all of the primary connections are vertical, management-services have a tendency to form into hierarchies and silos. This is a natural *and necessary* consequence of these interfaces: the only key point to bear in mind is that the hierarchies are not the whole of the story.

The management-services also have secondary *horizontal* interfaces with coordination-services and pervasive-services. These interfaces are described in more detail in the respective sections of the book: see Chapter 7, "Principles – Coordination Services," and Chapter 8, "Principles – Pervasive Services."

# Into Practice

- What management services exist in your enterprise? How would you distinguish between the different types of services at different layers of the enterprise?

- What happens to your perception of management in general when you choose to view them as *services*, rather than as mechanisms of control? What happens when you view each not as "a thing apart," something inherently "special and different" – as in the Taylorist machine-metaphor – but as just another type of service delivered to the enterprise?

- By what means are the system-5 services – purpose, policy, and identity – defined in your enterprise? In what ways – if at all – is that process of definition distributed throughout the enterprise?

- In what ways and by what means are the *expression* of policy and identity distributed through the enterprise? Would you be able to use the term "celebrated" to describe that policy and purpose, or does it seem more that it's something *imposed* on the rest of the enterprise by senior management? If the latter, what impact does this have on the enterprise as a whole? What, if necessary, could or should you do to change this?

- By what means are the system-4 services – business-intelligence, strategy, market-knowledge, and the like – defined and determined in your enterprise? In what ways – if at all – are those processes distributed throughout the enterprise, or are those responsibilities and capabilities reserved to a specific team somewhere near the senior-management levels?

- In what ways and by what means are the *expression* of strategy and the like distributed through the enterprise? Is it codeveloped, "owned" throughout the enterprise, or does it seem more that it's something *imposed* on the rest of the enterprise by senior management? If the latter, what impact does this have on the enterprise as a whole? What, if necessary, could or should you do to change this?

- What detail-level tactics are used for direction and management of the "downstream" delivery-services? What requirements and criteria are passed down the tree? In what forms? How are the requisite resources identified, obtained, and distributed? What performance-metrics are passed back up from the downstream services? In what forms? How is the balance between requirements, resources, and performance identified, verified, and maintained? And in what ways, and by what transforms, are those performance-metrics aggregated to pass up the tree?

- How are the competing demands and priorities of policy, strategy, and tactics resolved within the management-services? How does this vary at different levels and in different areas of the enterprise?

- What differences can you see between the espoused values and priorities of the enterprise and the priorities which actually apply in practice? If "the purpose of the system is what it does," what is the *actual* "purpose" of the enterprise? In what ways does this vary at different levels and in different silos of the enterprise? What could you do, in architecture terms, to bring the espoused purpose and actual purpose into closer alignment?

- If management-services tend naturally to form hierarchies and silos, because of the nature of their interfaces and interdependencies, what advantages and disadvantages to the enterprise as a whole can you see arising from this fact? What could you do to address the disadvantages without impacting the advantages?

# Summary

In this chapter, we explored the role of the management-services in the overall system, which focus on information-flows and on the future of the enterprise. As such, they represent the "brain of the firm" – though for that reason may perhaps gain an excess amount of attention compared to the needs or natures of other service-types. Their interfaces tend naturally toward hierarchies and silo-structures, creating a risk of the "Taylorist trap" of overescalated issues, and sometimes also serious difficulties in coordination of end-to-end processes. These can be resolved by treating management not as "special and different," but as just another set of services within the overall enterprise – although in practice this shift can only happen with appropriate support right from the top.

In the next chapter, we will review the role of the coordination-services that maintain the connections across the enterprise.

# CHAPTER 7

# Principles – Coordination Services

In the service-oriented enterprise, coordination-services create and maintain relationships across the enterprise. Without them, the enterprise would literally fall apart, as there would be nothing to hold the various functional silos together as an integrated whole.

Coordination-services provide horizontal links that bridge the gaps – or chasms – between the silos. Although always founded in relationships of some kind, some form of cross-link *between* one thing or function or person and the next, the focus is also on what the enterprise *does* or *knows* – in contrast to the pervasive-services, which focus more on what the enterprise *is*.

---

Before we start work on any of this part of the architecture, we need to be aware that the politics here can be extraordinarily challenging – and we need to be careful about that fact. For example, the enterprise cannot function effectively without the coordination-services: they're the functional glue that holds everything together. But yet again we're likely to hit yet another Taylorist trap here, because middle-managers often hate those services, and hate them with a passion…

© Tom Graves 2023
T. Graves, *The Service-Oriented Enterprise*, https://doi.org/10.1007/978-1-4842-9189-4_7

Coordination-services are horizontal, which immediately is anathema to the vertical orientation of the management-services. By definition, they operate *between* silos and hence seem to be outside of any ordinary manager's control. By insisting on cross-functional effectiveness over local efficiency, generalists may disrupt individual managers' personal performance-targets – which can hit hard on performance-based bonuses. And almost all performance-metrics are both vertical and function-specific, which means that the more the cross-functional generalists do their real work, the less they appear to do. Often, the only way to measure generalists' performance is at the level of the whole – hence, that authority would have to pass right up the hierarchy, far "above" where the generalists themselves might work, reinforcing the managers' grievances against apparent "insubordination." So overall, the managers' hatred is often understandable, even if not actually appropriate, but it's not a happy mix…

There *are* a few coordination-services that have formally recognized business roles: the Program Management Office is one such example. But most generalists I know will hide behind blurry job-titles such as "communications officer" or "ideation manager," or operate as a "skunk-works" under the shelter of a powerful patron. Yet it's a risky tactic: when the patron goes, so does the protection, and as one sardonic senior colleague put it, "if you're not being fired at least once every couple of years, you're probably not doing your job properly!"

A better solution is to break out of the Taylorist trap by showing that the problem comes from Taylorism itself – its arbitrary assumption that the vertical orientation of management alone is what makes the enterprise work. In other words, the problems that we see here come from the structure, rather than the people, so none of this is anyone's fault: there's no-one to blame. Yes, of course, those vertical management-services do matter, but we need a better *balance* between vertical and horizontal. And we can create that by showing that the coordination-services do exist – and *need* to exist – and also what they actually *do* as the enterprise "glue-logic." We need real job-titles for cross-functional generalists, proper recognition for their roles at every level of the enterprise, and real *horizontal* performance-metrics for them, too. A proper balance between local efficiency and overall effectiveness in managers' performance-based bonuses would also help, because that might take some of the heat – and hurt – out of the argument. We hope, anyway.

Do be aware, though, that the politics around these kinds of change will always be hard: to have any chance of getting it right, we'll definitely need the full support of the CEO and executive, and the authority and permission to go anywhere and talk with anyone that we need.

---

Note that for our purposes here, for enterprise-architecture, the *form* that the coordination-service takes is less important than that it exists, and that such coordination takes place at all. IT can usually help in this, but it's not the only option, and not necessarily the best option either. For example, typical people-roles for coordination-services might include

- Cross-functional bodies such as Program Management Office

- Troubleshooters and multiskilled maintenance-crews

- Individual cross-functional generalists

- "Linkers" and "fixers" for end-to-end processes

- "Supernodes" in enterprise social-networks

Coordination may also occur through knowledge-sharing tools and techniques – some formal, some informal – such as

- Interservice schedule-meetings and scheduling-systems

- Shared standards

- Shared glossary and thesaurus

- Conferences and cross-functional meetings

- Wikis, emails, and social-network software

- Online and offline collaboration tools

The services will typically take on one of three distinct roles, each aligned to one of the three types of management-services:

- *"Develop the business"*: Aligns with "policy," VSM system-5

- *"Change the business"*: Aligns with "strategy," VSM system-4

- *"Run the business"*: Aligns with "direction," VSM system-3

Although the business-roles may differ, the overall structure and function of each type is the same in each case.

# Viable System Context

In viable-system terms, these are the *VSM system-2* services.

In VSM diagrams, as shown in Figure 7-1, these are represented by an upward-pointing triangle.

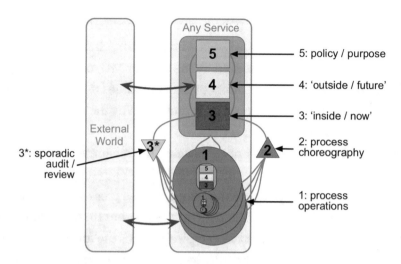

***Figure 7-1.***  *VSM "systems"*

In the tetradian architecture-model, these typically represent the *relational* dimension, often intersecting with the *conceptual* dimension as the sharing of personal tacit knowledge or narrative knowledge.

In the organism-metaphor, these represent the "superorganism" emergent-communication mechanisms for the enterprise – not yet fully understood in current biological sciences, but known to exist, for example, in insect social-systems such as beehives and ant-nests, in polymorphic entities such as slime-molds, and in how trees communicate with each other across a whole forest.

# Enterprise Context

In top-level VSM diagrams, coordination-services would usually be represented by a single system-2 triangle connected to the main management-services rectangle, although sometimes this may be split into separate system-2 instances for each of the three distinct management-services types.

At the board-level, "develop the business" coordination would always be represented by the CEO or MD; coordination for "change the business" would typically also be represented by the CEO or MD, or sometimes by an explicit role of Chief Strategy Officer or Chief Change Officer; while "run the business" coordination would be represented by the COO, or even – if perhaps inappropriately – by the CFO.

In the body of the organization, "develop the business" coordination will typically occur in the uppermost levels of the hierarchy-tree as interpersonal and intergroup relationships, and as cross-functional events or "suggestion box"–style tools and techniques rather than by explicit roles. "Change the business" coordination typically takes the form of projects and project-teams, and more broadly by a dedicated Program Management Office or equivalent. "Run the business" coordination will be represented by a few explicit roles, probably supplemented by more covert roles and by shared responsibilities and personal connections across the silos.

# Subunits or Variants

As described earlier, coordination-services have three variations in role: "develop the business," "change the business," and "run the business." Despite the differences in role, all three have essentially the same internal function and structure.

# Develop the Business

This assists in the development and dissemination of policy, requirements and imperatives, and enterprise vision, values, and identity – anything to do with the nature of the business and the principles that guide development and change. To do this, these services connect with the "conversation" between the management services "policy" and "strategy" (VSM system-5 and system-4).

Typical examples include

- Business architecture and whole-of-enterprise architecture

- Cross-functional policy and standards committees

- Policy-development events, particularly "large-group interventions" such as Future Search and Open Space Technology – see Appendix B, "Resources."

---

There's also some intersection here with the role of the pervasive-services, but it's important to realize that they're not the same.

The key difference is one of direction or emphasis, illustrated by the respective symbols on VSM diagrams; as can be seen in Figure 7-1, the coordination-services triangle points up, while the pervasive-services triangle points down. The "develop the business" coordination-services help ideas about policy, identity, and overall direction to "bubble upward" from anywhere in the enterprise, whereas pervasive-services are more about working downward to develop awareness of the *practical* implications of enterprise values, and capabilities to support and validate alignment with those values.

More on that in the next chapter; see Chapter 8, "Principles – Pervasive Services."

---

Middle-managers may well regard these services as irrelevant to their operations, "just stuff for head-office idiots," and so on. Don't be surprised if you hear sarcastic comments about "time-wasting nuisances" and the like, or throwaway remarks that "some people have *real* work to do, y'know?" Some of these may conceal subtle fears about threats to managers' authority, about bypassing "the proper channels"; such fears are understandable, and *do* need to be respected, if perhaps carefully *not* acknowledged in public...

---

Once more, the business-politics are really crucial for all of this – so again, we're going to need the full support of the CEO and executive here if we're to make it work. This is another reason why enterprise-architecture in particular needs to be set up right from the start to report to the whole executive, and *not* merely placed several layers down below the CIO or CTO.

---

The point is that, whether middle-managers like it or not, these processes do need to happen at *every* level of the enterprise. If they don't, there's no way to access the detail-level knowledge that arises from cross-functional interactions at the point of delivery and above – which would lead us straight back to the Taylorist trap again. We also risk losing people's engagement in the identity and purpose of the enterprise – and that engagement is something that is literally vital to the long-term viability of the enterprise.

One of our tasks as enterprise-architects, then, is to ensure that any systems we develop to support this will be available *everywhere* in the enterprise – and that senior management mandate and authorize the systems' use by everyone, too.

## Change the Business

This assists with coordination between the various stakeholders in any cross-functional change-project – a new capability, a changed business-process, or whatever. To do this, it connects with the conversation between the management-services for "strategy" and for "direction" (VSM system-4 and system-3) in the respective service-delivery layers.

Typical examples include

- Project Office and Program Management Office

- Process-architecture, IT-architecture, and other domain-architectures

- Project teams and business-transformation teams

- Capability-development teams

- Training and skills-development

---

As enterprise architects, we'll probably have least problems with middle-managers over this category of coordination-services, compared to the other two. Given the way it disrupts the steady-state assumptions of existing processes, change-management may still be viewed as something of an evil, but at least as an unavoidable and possibly even necessary evil!

---

# Run the Business

This connects with the vertical communications "down" and "up" between the "direction" management-service (VSM system-3) and its "child" delivery-services (VSM system-1) to guide coordination between delivery-services for end-to-end business-processes.

Typical examples include

- Intersilo scheduling systems

- Whole-of-process dashboards and process-flow models

- Real-time critical-path analysis

- Troubleshooters with formal authority to bridge silos

- Knowledge-sharing systems such as wikis, best-practice reference-systems, "problem boards"

- Process-choreography both within the organization and beyond with customers and suppliers

Most of these services will be people-based or IT-based, or some combination of the two, but a few may be entirely mechanical. A classic example of the latter is the old "token"-based safety-interlock for single-line operation of a railway, which still has its counterparts in modern manufacturing.

The main work of these services is *inter*silo, to facilitate end-to-end processes. Coordination *within* a silo is usually the role and responsibility of the "direction" management-service (system-3), though these services may also provide feedback to management on interservice scheduling and conflicts between those respective "child"-services.

---

Note, though, that this implied dual-responsibility for coordination of "child" services provides plenty of opportunity for clashes and conflicts between the vertically oriented managers and the horizontally oriented end-to-end link-roles. Such clashes occur often in organizational cultures that place an overemphasis on managers' need to be "in control" at all times. In such cases, proceed with caution – because if we're not careful, here be dragons, breathing fire and fury!

Making that link-function explicit will help, likewise emphasizing that it's just feedback, helping to keep everything on track at a whole-of-enterprise level, not criticism or attack about "failure to control." In short, it's business-politics again, with all that that implies; the term "stakeholder management" might usefully come to mind here, perhaps especially when we remember that a stakeholder is anyone who wields a sharp-pointed stake in our direction, and there can be a lot more of those than we might like! So for the enterprise architect, care is the watchword here, coupled with well-honed people-skills – that and also respect for the real difficulties faced by each side in this equation.

# Interfaces

Coordination-services have symmetrical *horizontal* connections, as both **provider** and **requester**, to each of their "customer" delivery-services for which they provide coordination. These connections may be modeled either as information-flows coordinating traffic and activities between the "customer" delivery-services or as the interface itself between those delivery-services.

As described earlier, and illustrated in Figure 7-2, these connections will link to each "customer" as follows:

- *"Develop the business"*: Bridge between "policy" and "strategy" management-services

- *"Change the business"*: Bridge between "strategy" and "direction" management-services

- *"Run the business"*: Bridge between "direction" management-service and any or all of its "child" delivery-services

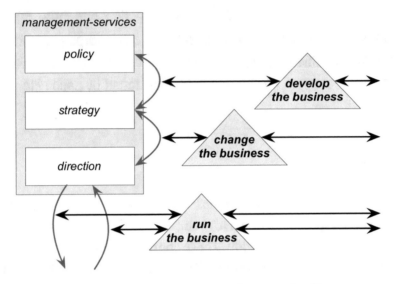

**Figure 7-2.** *Coordination services: interfaces with other systems*

Coordination-services will also have a symmetric pair of *vertical* connections, similar to those for the management-services set, linking "upward" into an appropriate point in the overall management-hierarchy, such as

- *"Develop the business"*: Sometimes further up the same branch, more often an almost direct link to a separate subbranch high up in the tree

- *"Change the business"*: Usually a link to the matching next level up in a parallel branch dedicated to business change, such as a Program Management Office program-to-project-to-task management-hierarchy

- *"Run the business"*: Usually a link to the next level up in the same branch of the hierarchy-tree

The VSM specification shows the system-2 coordination-service only as an upward connection to its system-3 management-service and sideways to some or all of that service's "child" system-1 delivery-services. Some VSM variants label this as "regulation and tactical planning," though other terms are sometimes used. In effect, this is a "run the business" coordination, but one in which the link is more *within* a single silo – a special-case, in contrast to the more generic usage for the three distinct coordination-service roles, and for intrasilo *and* intersilo integration.

## Into Practice

- What coordination-services exist within your enterprise? What forms do they take? What "glue-logic" functions do they perform within the enterprise?

- Which – if any – of the coordination-services are formally recognized within the enterprise structure? For those services which do not have such recognition, how do they operate? From where do they obtain their resources?

- What performance-metrics are applied to coordination-services? If there are any, what weighting is assigned to local vs. global or whole-of-enterprise effectiveness, in that assessment of personal or team performance?

- What clashes – if any – exist between management-services and coordination-services? If such clashes occur, what forms do they take, and which side tends to "win" each argument? Who – and at what level – has the authority to act as arbiter in such clashes? And what are the consequences of any such clash?

- What distinctions do you see between coordination-services for "run the business," "change the business," and "develop the business"? What different forms do they take? Are some of these represented only at specific levels of the enterprise? What changes – if any – would be needed to ensure that they are represented at every level of the enterprise?

- As an enterprise-architect, how would you represent such cross-functional services in process-models, service-models, and function-models for the enterprise? How would you map the information-needs and process-flows for such services?

# Summary

In this chapter, we explored the role of coordination-services and their relationships with other types of services. For example, where management-services build vertical hierarchies and silos within the enterprise, the coordination-services bridge *across* the silos, creating links for end-to-end processes and enabling cross-functional integration. The services typically provide coordination in three distinct yet related areas: the routine running of business processes, changes to the business structure and capabilities, and changes to the overall purpose and direction of the business. The enterprise cannot operate without such services, though few will be formally recognized in management structures – an issue which itself can have serious impacts on enterprise effectiveness.

In the next chapter, we'll review the pervasive-services that help to maintain quality throughout every part of the enterprise.

# CHAPTER 8

# Principles – Pervasive Services

In the service-oriented enterprise, the pervasive-services manage what the enterprise *is*. If, to quote Beer, the management-services represent "the brain of the firm," the pervasive-services in a sense represent its heart or its soul.

---

Once again, we'd best take some care to avoid "the religion bit" here! Some types of enterprise – particularly charities and not-for-profit organizations – might well use the term "soul" in this context, but for most of us, it's the principle behind that term that's more relevant. And the principle here is that of values and vision and policy and the like as the anchor or "guiding star" for the enterprise, as described earlier in the subsection "Policy, Purpose, and Identity" in Chapter 6, "Principles – Management Services." Pervasive-services hold us to the anchor, or keep us on-track to that guiding-star; that's really all we're talking about here. If terms such as "soul" are a problem, don't use 'em! – use whatever else works, as long as it does illustrate that key principle.

---

© Tom Graves 2023
T. Graves, *The Service-Oriented Enterprise*, https://doi.org/10.1007/978-1-4842-9189-4_8

A service *serves* some purpose, something, or someone, but what, or whom, does it serve? *How* does it serve? By what means does it ensure that it *does* serve? Such questions might perhaps sound somewhat abstract, but they're actually right at the core of service-orientation and the service-oriented enterprise.

To keep track on some purpose, there are three distinct aspects that we'll need:

- Develop *awareness* that the purpose exists

- Develop *capability* to serve that purpose

- *Review* to audit and verify that we have indeed served that purpose

Somewhere in the middle, we'll also need to *use* that capability so as to serve the purpose, but the other types of services – delivery, management, and coordination – already handle those concerns. Here, with the pervasive-services, we're concerned with just those three subthemes: awareness, capability, and review.

Some common business-examples of pervasive themes include the following:

- Quality – including exception-handling, issue-tracking, corrective-action, and process-improvement

- Privacy, security, and trust

- Health, safety, and environment

- Ethics, social-responsibility, and legal compliance

- Cost-effectiveness and waste minimization

- Knowledge-sharing and innovation

- Whole-of-enterprise efficiency and effectiveness

They're described as "pervasive" themes because they need to pervade *every* part of the enterprise, to embed them into the core of every activity – in effect as a way of life, in the business sense. The pervasive-services need to exist in order to promulgate those themes throughout the enterprise; for example, simply stating that "such-and-such is an enterprise value" is not going to do anything useful at all – we need to *do* something to make it happen. People need to be told not just that these are the values, but they also need to know *why* those values exist, what purpose those values serve, and so on. We need to create and maintain capabilities that will support those values – otherwise, there's no *means* to support them. And performance-metrics need to be defined for every one of these themes – otherwise, we can't review them or guide continuous improvement on them.

---

Although it sometimes needs a bit of sideways-thinking to do it, we can also embed those values into processes, into software, and into *every* activity.

To give a real example, one of our banking clients had a project to redesign the cash-management in their branches and ATMs. The aim was to reduce the bank's overall cash-holdings by ten percent – a nontrivial target, but achievable – in a way that would support enterprise values around effectiveness and financial performance, but also respect the skills and experience of individual staff.

What they wanted was to achieve a better balance between central control – the "big picture" view – and local knowledge, which warned about unusual ebbs and flow in cash-handling from fairs and markets and other local events. To tackle that, we created a forecasting system that garnered and combined all the different types of knowledge about events and the like, giving appropriate weightings to each.

We also needed to dissuade a common habit by bank-branches of ordering cash only at the last minute – which was not only expensive but sometimes led to empty ATMs and even empty branches. So we changed the existing cash-order system to a much simpler "today's to-do list," with all the day's essential activities already scheduled for the branches on their opening screen. The old overused emergency-order process, which in the previous system was almost the first item that the bank-staff saw, did still exist – but the screen to access it was now three layers down. It's a simple and *practical* way to persuade people to change behaviors in line with purpose: not by bullying or cajoling, but by making it *easier* for them to do it right, and harder to do it wrong.

---

We can, and probably should, use the existing formal standards wherever practicable to guide the design and implementation of pervasive-services. Note, though, that these will each have their own emphases, covering different aspects of the issues: in quality-management, for example, ISO-9000 ensures that the capabilities exist in the enterprise, but Six Sigma ensures that they're *used*!

In principle, we *can* operate the enterprise without any pervasive-services, but it certainly won't operate effectively, and probably won't operate for long, either. There needs to be an *explicit* purpose, an *explicit* vision and values, and a systematic means to manage legal compliance and the rest, because if we don't have these, what we get instead is POSIWID – the purpose of the system is what it does – and we probably won't like what it does at all... In that sense, the pervasive-services *matter*.

We also need to beware of what we might call "antiservices": concerns such as absenteeism, presenteeism, destructive rumor-mongering, and so on. These invariably sabotage the intended purpose – if there is one – and will certainly damage enterprise effectiveness wherever they occur. Technically speaking, they're not likely to be part of our responsibility as enterprise-architects, but there's plenty we can do to dissuade such happenings, as in the ATM example earlier. Do what we can, really.

# Viable System Context

In viable-system terms, these are the **VSM system-3\*** services – or rather, system-3\*, "sporadic audit," is just one example of a much broader category of pervasive-services.

In VSM diagrams, as shown in Figure 8-1, these are represented by a downward-pointing triangle.

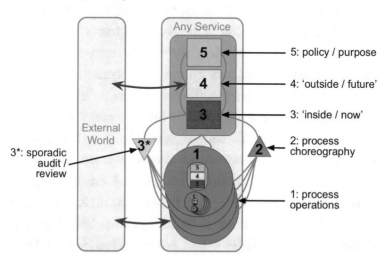

***Figure 8-1.*** *VSM "systems"*

In the tetradian architecture-model, these typically represent the *aspirational* dimension.

In the organism-metaphor, these represent distributed glandular communication systems – the endocrine-system hormones and suchlike – of the enterprise.

# Enterprise Context

It is probable that a top-level VSM diagram would aggregate all of the pervasive-services into a single system-3* entity, represented by a downward-pointing triangle linked to the system-5 "policy" management-service.

At the board-level, all the pervasive-services should – nominally, at least – be represented by the CEO or MD, as the person formally responsible for defining and preserving enterprise identity and for promulgating all its policies, principles, and values. In practice, some of those responsibilities may be taken on by other senior executives, such as the CFO for financial audit. Other examples might include the Chief Information Officer (CIO) or Chief Knowledge Officer (CKO) for knowledge sharing, or a possible Chief Security Officer for security-issues – the exact roles and requirements would vary from one enterprise to another.

In the body of the organization, the key responsibilities for development of awareness and capability for a pervasive theme would typically be assigned to a small team of "evangelists" such as a health and safety unit, with the authority to act and interact with any part of the enterprise. Responsibilities for audit on that theme may be assigned either to the same team or to a separate team: financial audit is one obvious example where such separation may be mandated by law. Overall, though, responsibilities for each pervasive theme are necessarily shared and owned by *everyone*; by definition, the theme must pervade *every* aspect of the entire enterprise.

This shared-responsibility applies not only within the bounds of the organization but extends also to all parts of the shared enterprise that are beyond the bounds of the organization itself. For example, concerns about quality or security will *necessarily* extend to suppliers and outsourced service-providers: the SCOR standard for supply-chain management extends at the least from the supplier's supplier to the customer's customer, while US legislation mandates control of the use of some types of materiel all the way to the endpoint of use, regardless of the number of intervening steps. Governance becomes much more complex as soon as it extends beyond organization boundaries, but engagement in a given market or social context – a given "vision" – will mandate that some themes must pervade everywhere in that context and hence will apply to all roles and services in that shared enterprise; the architecture of the enterprise *must* support this requirement, however difficult the governance may be in practice.

## Subunits or Variants

As described earlier, there may be many different types of pervasive services in the enterprise, addressing a very wide range of potential themes; yet each service – or service-set – should present essentially the same overall structure.

The three key subthemes in pervasive-services – creation of awareness of the issues, development of skills and capability, and verification and audit – may sometimes be bundled into the same overall service, but would more often be delivered separately. In some cases, separation may be mandated by law or regulation: this would typically be the case for formal auditing and for certification of skills-development. Hence, in some models, it may be useful to distinguish between the different subservice types, perhaps by color-coding, but the same downward-pointing triangle as shown in Figure 8-1 should be used as the base-symbol in each case.

# Interfaces

As shown in Figure 8-2, pervasive-services have three distinct symmetrical connections, as both **provider** and **requester**, with each of their "customer" services.

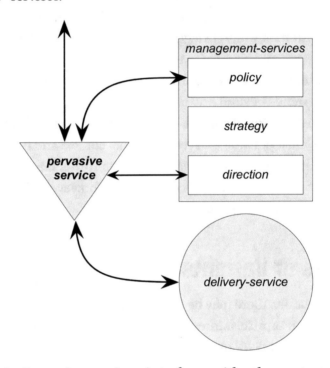

***Figure 8-2.*** *Pervasive services: interfaces with other systems*

As in previous chapters, what follows might at first look like "too much theory" – but again, though, for enterprise-architecture there's a really important practical question here: How do we get the enterprise-values to thread through *everything* that the organization is and does?

That's what this section is about: we have to connect up to the place in the organization that manages policy, purpose, identity, and meaning, and we then have to connect that all the way down into real-time action. We'll then use the ordinary management-tasks to make sure that this happens in the way that we need, so that people know *why* each policy and value is important, know *how* to apply those in their everyday work, actually *do* it in practice, and then learn from what they've done, to continually improve that practice.

It's described in the following VSM terms, so that it fits with the rest of the service-model structure that we're building here – but if you're ever in doubt about what it all means and what it's for, check back with that preceding summary.

---

The first symmetric-pair connection is with the system-5 "policy" management-service, either at the same level – at the top of the hierarchy-tree – or else *at the next level above,* for any pervasive-service instance below that top level. This is a "requirements downward/reporting upward" relationship, similar to that for coordination-services or the upward link of a management-services set.

The second symmetric-pair link is with the system-3 "direction" management-service at the same level. This is primarily for task-coordination, *not* authorization or reporting: in particular, it's essential that an audit-service is *not* controlled or managed by the service being audited, as that would defeat the whole object of the audit.

---

In this sense, the VSM label "system-3*" is a bit of a misnomer – instead, it really ought to be "system-5*," to indicate that the primary connection is to the "policy" management-service. It's probably best to leave the current label alone, though, to avoid breaking any existing use of the VSM elsewhere in the enterprise.

---

The third symmetric-pair connection is with any or all of the "child" delivery-services at the current level. This link delivers the service-content and reporting for the pervasive-service and hence will vary with each type of pervasive-service, and the details of the content-type delivered – typically either a review or audit of some kind, issue-awareness development, or capability-development.

Note that, as with the coordination-services, this differs somewhat from the description in the VSM specification, where system-3* is shown as connecting to the system-3 "direction" service. The key reason for the change here is that, as Patrick Hoverstadt explains in his book on the VSM, system-3* audit *must bypass a management level* in order to do a proper audit of the underlying context of that management-level. The same applies for other pervasive-services: as expressions *of* policy, the primary authority should come from system-5 "policy"; the role here of the system-3 "direction" services – the everyday middle-management or line-management tasks – is simply to make sure that everything that needs to get done to support the work of the pervasive-services does indeed get done.

---

Remember that ultimately all of this is about the detail of service-design: the connections between the different types of services, and the information and other flows that move across those connections. We'll see more on how all of that works in practice in the next sections of the book.

---

# Into Practice

- What purpose does the enterprise serve? What vision does it hold? What values?

- What policies, regulations, law, and other social expectations apply to the enterprise from outside?

- What means would be required to keep the enterprise "on track" to serve each of those chosen or imposed imperatives? What means would be required to ensure that those imperatives are known and understood throughout the enterprise? What means to increase enterprise capabilities to serve those imperatives? What means to report and verify that the enterprise as a whole does indeed serve those imperatives?

- If "the purpose of the system is what it does," what *actual* imperatives does the enterprise serve? Does this vary in different areas of the enterprise – and if so, by how much? Overall, how much, and in what ways, do these "actual imperatives" differ from the espoused purpose and values? If a gap exists, what services would be needed to close that gap – and also to ensure that it does not reopen?

- What "antiservices" can you identify in the enterprise? What *architectural* means could you use to minimize their activities and impact?

- In what ways could and should the pervasive-services themselves be monitored? Who watches the watchers?

# Summary

In this chapter, we explored how the pervasive-services help to guide and ensure quality throughout the enterprise, covering themes such as safety, security, service quality, and corporate social-responsibility. They extend the enterprise imperatives from the topmost "policy" management-service through to every part of the entire enterprise, all the way down to the smallest detail. One specific example, as described in the VSM, is sporadic audit, to verify reported results against actual activity. In practice, though, there would usually need to be a much broader range of equivalent pervasive-services, to guide the review, audit, and continual improvement relative to all of the other enterprise principles, policies, and values – and also create awareness of the issues, and the capabilities needed to support those themes throughout the enterprise.

In the next chapter, we'll assess how the various types of services need to interact with each other and the principles and patterns that can guide designs to ensure that these interactions will occur correctly.

# CHAPTER 9

# Principles – Properties and Patterns

As we've seen in previous chapters, there are many different types of services, each type with its own specific role within the enterprise-as-a-service. But perhaps the most crucial point is that no service exists in isolation: it is *always* part of a larger system, hence systems within systems within systems, all the way up to "the everything."

---

To emphasize the living-enterprise metaphor again, perhaps that ought to be an *ecosystem* rather than a "system." The latter term tends to push us back to the old machine-metaphor, which really does start to show its limitations when we get to this level of complexity.

Looking back at that list of characteristics of an IT-based service-oriented architecture (see the initial section in Chapter 2, "Basics – Service-Oriented Architecture"), it's clear they make even more sense as views into an ecosystem. Loose-coupling allows a system to adapt and optimize itself to the conditions within its broader ecosystem, and allows the ecosystem itself to adapt to *its* changing context.

© Tom Graves 2023
T. Graves, *The Service-Oriented Enterprise*, https://doi.org/10.1007/978-1-4842-9189-4_9

Each entity within the ecosystem is interchangeable, though only in the sense that the system itself also changes with each change of its component members.

And in a living ecosystem, ultimately *everything* is recomposable and reusable, if only as a compost: in software, as in nature, each new generation builds on the foundations provided by its predecessors. Yet there's also a very interesting shift in perspective that occurs when we rethink the relationships in an ecosystem's food-chain in terms of services: What services are rendered from prey to predator? – or for that matter, from predator to prey? Kind of eye-opening when we apply that reframing to our own business-ecosystem, too…

---

To make sense of all this complexity, we need to turn to systems-theory. What it's really about is identifying impacts on the *effectiveness* of the overall system. Yet while the full version of systems-theory can be intensely mathematical, to the extent of being almost impenetrable to anyone other than academics, we can reduce the core down to a set of five principles that *are* simple enough to apply in business practice. In our own work, we described these as the $R^5$ principles:

- *Rotation*: Review a context from multiple perspectives.

- *Reciprocation*: Balance in transactions between services and across the whole ecosystem.

- *Resonance*: Feedback-loops and the like.

- *Recursion*: Patterns of how themes recur at different scales.

- *Reflexion*: The whole can be seen in every part.

*Rotation* is perhaps the most straightforward of these principles: for example, we use it every time we work our way through a checklist, such as this list itself. Those four categories of services – delivery, management, coordination, and pervasives – and their respective subtypes, variants, and interrelationships provide probably the most valuable rotation for our purposes here.

*Reciprocation* means that everything has to balance out somehow. The catch is that this balance may not be direct or immediate, and in many cases may only be achieved over time and over the entire ecosystem, with transfers that can sometimes shift between the physical, conceptual, relational, and aspirational dimensions.

---

Reciprocation in systems also highlights another serious concern at a much larger scale of business. Our current economic model ultimately relies on an assumption of infinite growth: the catch is that this isn't possible in a closed system – even if that "system" is as large as an entire planet. In the ecological sense, our so-called "economy" is not a *viable system*, in any sense of the term.

To be precise, it's in effect a gigantic "pyramid game" – and pyramid-games can only function for as long as new resources can be pulled in at the base. Ecological analysis suggests that our economy passed that point at least 50 years ago: there's certainly no doubt now that it's far overrun its available resources, and that what's left is little more than a shared delusion that's getting more dangerous by the day. Ouch…

So while our immediate concern here is the system of an individual enterprise, expect there to be an increasingly rough ride from the broader ecosystem within which our enterprise will operate. There's more on the business implications of this, and how to address those implications, in the book *Power and Response-ability: The Human Side of Systems* – see Appendix B, "Resources."

---

**Resonance** would be a favorite theme for almost every systems-theory practitioner. Reciprocation tells us that the system has to balance out somehow; but in reality it often does so not in simple win/lose transactions, but in resonant loops that amplify or damp down the resultant feedback. To complicate the transactions even further, there are often delays in those feedback loops that can range in timescale from microseconds to millennia. Although business concerns are likely to be in more visible timescales, from seconds to years, as architects we'll often need to be able to map out those resonant effects to any or every timescale, so as to be able to see what's actually going on.

**Recursion** is one of the most valuable items in the systems-theory toolkit. Patterns of relationship or interaction repeat or are "self-similar" at different scales: the "org-chart" is one obvious example, and the extended "viable systems" model we're exploring here is another. Whether the system is a low-level software, a mid-level process, or an entire enterprise, it's always worthwhile watching out for any possible recursion, because it makes our designs much simpler to describe, define, and implement.

**Reflexion** is a somewhat bizarre corollary of recursion, in that in a recursive system, the nature of the whole is also reflected in any and all of its constituent parts. The vision and values of an enterprise, its policies and purpose, echo all the way down to individual services and subservices and sub-subservices – or need to do so, otherwise what we get is POSIWID. This is where the pervasive-services come into the enterprise picture, and why they are so important to the operation of the enterprise as a whole. But the flipside of this is that wherever we see recursion, we don't have to try to analyze the whole system: we can find out much of its nature just from looking at any part – which again greatly helps to simplify both design and verification that our designs will actually work in the real world.

And that's the aim of viewing services as systems: it gives us a means to improve overall *effectiveness*: efficient, reliable, elegant, appropriate, and integrated as an effective enterprise.

# Service Quality

In service-analysis and design, it's all too easy to focus so much on the functional requirements that we forget to pay attention to the so-called "nonfunctional" ones. And that can be a *big* mistake...

---

"Nonfunctional requirement" is an amazing misnomer of a term that's a hangover from the long-forgotten days of functional-programming for mainframes. All that "nonfunctional" means is that it's a requirement that is not specifically about function. Yet it kind of gives the impression that these are the requirements that don't do anything and therefore don't matter. But that's a serious mistake, because a more accurate term is "*qualitative* requirements" – requirements about quality.

And qualities, and *quality*, most certainly *do* matter in service-design. A service-level agreement is essentially about the quality of service. Service-management is mostly about the quality of service. The pervasive-services are all about quality in the enterprise. In a competitive environment, an enterprise survives by quality – even price, because price itself is a "nonfunctional" quality. Quality *matters*.

---

One of the difficulties here is that while we can indeed describe some qualities in quantitative terms, that isn't the case for all – and yet we need to treat all of the requirements in the same way, or at least to the same level of detail. Often, the only way to establish or evaluate a nonnumeric quality is through skill and experience – which implies the need for a real person somewhere in the service loop. But in IT-centric contexts, especially where there's a drive to use IT primarily for cost-cutting rather than to improve the overall effectiveness of a process, there's often a tendency to hide from

119

this fact, or to assume that the IT can handle everything – which it can't. If that does happen, there's no way to maintain quality: hence either a poor-quality service or a service that fails without warning, apparently at random, with no way to see how or why. Quality needs to be designed in from the beginning – and designed in *as* quality.

One way to think about quality, or qualit*ies*, is in terms of the pervasive-services. Each of the pervasives represents a "nonfunctional requirement" that must be expressed in *everything* in the enterprise: every service must include appropriate support for the security requirements, the environmental requirements, the health and safety requirements, and so on.

---

In practice, the pervasives *define* what "quality" *is* for the enterprise. That's *why* they're so important – and also why it's so disturbing, and so worrying, that they're so little referenced in most current enterprise-architectures and enterprise structures or in most other business-methods, for that matter…

---

We also need to think about quality over the longer term. There's another tendency to think of services only in terms of design-time, as if there's a single static "*the* service," part of the machine: but in reality, each service has its own life-cycle within the living enterprise. Every part of that life-cycle spins off other services to serve the needs at that specific point: hence, for example, that category of services described earlier as "change the business" coordination-services. And every business capability will need some form of maintenance: for software, it might be an upgrade; for a manual process, it may mean training; for a machine, it may just be a quick check-over and a drop of oil here and there; but in every case, that too will mean more systems, more services.

A machine doesn't know about quality. It just *is* – and it's maintained from outside itself. A machine the size of an entire enterprise soon becomes far too complicated to manage: in short, it becomes impossible, hence the inevitability there of "wicked problems" for which there seems to be no possible solution, no matter how hard we try to control them.

But a living organism *does* know about quality – and hence can maintain itself, choose its direction, and adapt itself to changes in its environment and ecosystem. Hence, in turn, in its analogue of the living enterprise. When the interdependencies become impossibly complex, that emphasis on quality may be the only way we'll stay sane... In the service-oriented enterprise, quality *matters*.

# Service Interdependence

If quality guides our interpretation of interdependencies between services, that interdependence is what enables quality. In a sense, pervasiveness *is* interdependence: a quality is spread through the enterprise by those interdependencies and interconnections. The same is true for infrastructure: while the pervasives focus on the "is" of the enterprise, the infrastructures are coordination-services that sit *between* delivery-services and the like and provide support for what the enterprise does, what it knows, and how it relates. Each will touch *everywhere*: each often seemingly almost invisible, yet everything in the enterprise will depend on them.

---

There's what at first will seem an interesting dilemma here, in that an explicit aim of IT service-orientation, for example, is to minimize cross-dependencies. That's what "black-box" encapsulation is all about.

But it's not quite the dilemma it seems, because what we're doing here is *exposing* the interfaces to infrastructure and the pervasives – making the "invisible" visible. That then gives us a new way to handle any necessary "hardwired" cross-dependencies: we change them into messages and suchlike that pass through the now-visible infrastructure – hence the importance of an "enterprise service-bus" in IT-SOA implementations, or for that matter a light-rail system of some kind to manage the services of a city's commute. Both work because there's "loose-coupling" through an infrastructure connection that in effect is actually hardwired.

Service-orientation is not a simple panacea: as in both of those examples, there are several kinds of overhead involved in using the infrastructure; bandwidth can be a real problem; and for some infrastructures, creating point-to-point connections for everything can end up impossibly expensive. Relying too much on a single infrastructure can be risky, but duplication can again be too costly in too many ways. Plenty of trade-offs to consider there…

Yet a true service-orientation allows us to rethink the entire approach by which we might deliver a service. If we need the service of people at work, why do we insist that they must spend perhaps as much as a third of their working lives caught up in the miseries of the daily commute? Why not bring the work to them instead, via alternate infrastructures? That's a core principle behind software-as-a-service, in telecommuting, and in the piecework-assembly processes that are used in so many small manufacturing operations – and in the right contexts, it works very well indeed.

Done well, it also cuts costs all round. Yet in the longer term, we'll only maintain those savings if we include *all* the pervasive themes of the enterprise – quality-management, health-and-safety, security, and all of those other hidden services need to be in place too. So while service-orientation is probably essential for the viable enterprise, we need to do it right: a casual, careless, half-hearted approach to services can actually make it *less* viable – which would *not* be a good idea…

Other interdependencies needed for resilience and sustainability can seem more subtle. For example, the VSM indicates that every service must include subservices for its policy, strategy, direction, coordination, audit, and the like, as well as any number of "child" delivery-services. Unless these are built-in – which many won't be within, say, a detail-level IT web-service – then they need to be included by reference, as implied links to external services. Many such higher-level support-services – particularly for those within the implementation services at the detail-levels – would necessarily be provided by people, not IT. For example:

- Every service needs an *owner* – the person ultimately responsible for that service.

- Every service will probably need RACI matrices – lists of persons or roles responsible for, assists in, or to be consulted or informed about changes.

- Every service needs *version-identifiers* to support audit, quality management, change-management, and the like.

- Every service will probably need CRUD matrices – lists of persons, roles, or services that create, retrieve, update, or delete content through that service, or instances of the service itself.

- Every coordinating-service that sits between silos will need management support – in other words, links and transactions with the management-services – at the matching level in the respective silos.

- Every policy-service will need to link like-with-like to the matching policy-service in "parent"-and "child"-services up and down the hierarchy-trees – and likewise for strategy-services.

- Every pervasive-service must ultimately anchor to a declared quality, value, principle, or policy within the enterprise purpose.

From a design perspective, these are typical *patterns* that we would expect to see occurring recursively in many different forms at any level and in every aspect of the service-oriented enterprise.

Stafford Beer also asserted that every service might also need what he termed "algedonic" links that could connect with any – or even every – other service. These connections are effectively point-to-point, bypassing the usual communication-channels via the management hierarchy-trees.

---

In general, algedonic links should be reserved for emergencies only, in part because the requirement for point-to-point connections breaches the loose-coupling principle and could add enormous complexity to a system – though that concern is eased if a suitable infrastructure already exists to carry them, such as matching email, phone, and URL-address links to a help-desk service. "Algedonic" literally means "pain/pleasure"; hence, the "audit" component of the pervasive-services also acts as a kind of algedonic channel, identifying the respective type of "pain" or "pleasure" within the system.

Unsurprisingly, middle-managers often *hate* algedonic links: they bypass the formal trail of authority, and as a result may often seem *personally* threatening. But like it or not, such connections are *essential* to the viability of the service-oriented enterprise: the "normal channels" are invariably too slow to cope with emergencies, and without the algedonic links, the enterprise will crash and burn.

---

An article in *Scientific American* some years back described a variety of high-stress environments – electricity power-distribution and aircraft-carrier flight-deck were two of the examples – that all used exactly the same kind of management-structure. Each had a strict hierarchy of ranks and responsibilities: everyone knew their place, in every sense of that term – because that gave the greatest efficiency under "normal high-stress conditions." But at the same time, *everyone* was also able to connect with anyone else for emergency purposes: even the lowest-ranking erk on the aircraft-carrier had the authority *and duty* to call the admiral direct if they thought that the ship was at risk for any reason. Hence, it's neither a true rigid hierarchy nor a true "flat" management-structure, but a kind of "hierarchy/flat" somewhere in between, incorporating the best features of both and creating a *responsibility-driven* enterprise: that's what the algedonic links allow.

Following the same recursion, every link between services – every interdependency – is implicitly a link which also connects the physical, the conceptual, the relational, and the aspirational dimensions of the context: in other words, the things, knowledge, people, and purpose that apply in that context. Every link is about information; every link is about trust and about quality; and every link must exist in some form, physical, virtual, or otherwise.

This may at first sound somewhat abstract, but it has real practical implications for the service-oriented enterprise. For example, if every VSM link implies a need for some kind of information-transfer, the model is therefore also inherently a known proven pattern for IT-system design. The pervasive links in turn emphasize the importance of other key IT themes such as "database of record," "single sign-on," and "single source of truth" – often difficult to implement in practice, but all of them essential to overall quality in the service-oriented enterprise.

# Service Completeness

Another type of pattern we need to watch for is architectural *completeness*. To put it in its simplest form, services are usable to the extent that they're architecturally complete, yet also *re*usable to the extent that they're architecturally *in*complete. Given the natural recursion of services, we know that enterprise viability will depend on the presence of all the support-services and on the effectiveness of the interfaces between them. But to *reuse* services – that key concept of loose-coupling – we also need to be able to split them apart, to make services temporarily "incomplete."

- **Viability depends on completeness.**
  **Reuse depends on incompleteness.**

"Incomplete" services become design-patterns, or implementation-patterns. Those principles of loose-coupling and encapsulation are themselves design-patterns for intentional "incompletion," to be resolved at runtime: the connections and service-contracts create the completion needed to make service-delivery happen.

At this point, we need to link to another related architectural issue around completeness. A service is a combination of capability and function, yet this is only part of a more generic pattern for viable completeness at the implementation level:

- **"with *«asset»* do *«function»* at *«location»* using
  *«capability»* on *«event»* because *«decision»*"**

In principle, we should be able to describe the implementation-completeness of *everything* in terms of that one sentence-structure. It's derived from an expansion of the well-known Zachman framework, which extends the original with an extra row at the top for enterprise core-constants or "universals" and an extra dimension to clarify scope and actual implementation, as shown in Figure 9-1.

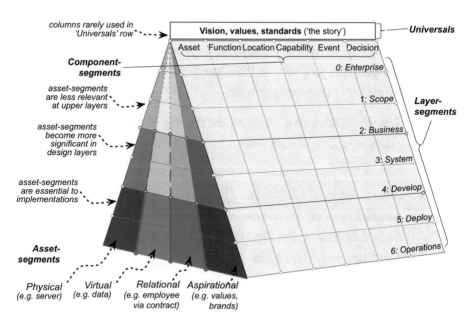

**Figure 9-1.** *Framework universals, rows, columns, and asset-segments*

---

The framework is described in more detail in a companion volume in this series, *Everyday Enterprise Architecture: Sensemaking, Strategy, Structures and Solutions* – see Appendix B, "Resources."

---

The "*Universals*" row represents a separate dimension, a kind of backplane to which *everything* must connect and align:

- *Universals*: Core constants for the overall shared-enterprise "story" such as vision, values, and standards to which everything should align – the key points of connection with enterprise partners and other stakeholders

For the vertical dimension of the framework, we partition scope in terms of timescale – a set of seven distinct layers or perspectives, from unchanging constants to items which change moment by moment. Each row adds another concern or attribute:

- *Row 0*: "**Enterprise**" – Identifies the key elements of the enterprise as a whole, within which the organization will operate

- *Row 1*: "**Scope**" (*Zachman*: "Planner") – Adds possibility of change, if usually slowly: core entities in each category, in list form, *without* relationships – the key "items of interest" for the enterprise

- *Row 2*: "**Business**" (*Zachman*: "Owner") – Adds relationships and dependencies between entities: core entities described in summary-form for business-metrics, including relationships between entities both of the same type ("primitives") and of different types ("composites")

- *Row 3*: "**System**" (*Zachman*: "Designer") – Adds attributes to abstract "logical" entities: entities expanded out into implementation-*independent* designs – includes descriptive attributes

- *Row 4*: "**Develop**" (*Zachman*: "Builder") – Adds details for real-world "physical" design: entities and attributes expanded out into implementation-*dependent* designs, including additional patterns such as cross-reference tables for "many-to-many" data-relationships

- *Row 5*: "**Deploy**" (*Zachman*: "Subcontractor" or "Out of Scope") – Adds details of intended future deployment: implementation of designs into actual software, actual business-processes, work-instructions, hardware, networks, etc.

- *Row 6*: "**Operations**" (*Zachman*: implied but not described) – Adds details of actual usage: specific instances of entities, processes, etc., as created, modified, and acted on in real-time operations

The rows also represent different categories of responsibilities or stakeholders, such as senior management responsible for "universals" and row 0 "enterprise," strategists at rows 1 and 2, architects and solution-designers at rows 3 and 4, and line managers and front-line staff at rows 5 and 6. In effect, this is the same layering that we see in the management-hierarchy, and in the nesting of abstract services.

Below the core "Universals," the framework splits horizontally into columns for six distinct categories of primitives, approximating to Zachman's what, how, where, who, when, and why:

- *What*: **Assets** of any kind – physical objects, data, links to people, morale, finances, etc.

- *How*: **Functions** – activities or services to create change, described independently from the agent (machine, software, person, etc.) that carries out that activity

- *Where*: **Locations** – in physical space (geography, etc.), virtual space (IP nodes, http addresses, etc.), relational space (social networks, etc.), time, and suchlike

- *Who*: **Capabilities** clustered as **roles** or "actors" – may be human, machine, software application, etc., and individual or collective

- *When*: **Events** and relationships between those events – may be in time, or physical, virtual, human, business-rule trigger, or other events

- *Why*: **Decisions**, reasons, constraints, and tests which trigger or validate the condition for the "reason," as in strategy, policy, business-requirements, business-rules, regulations, etc.

In the lower layers, we also need to split the columns themselves by context into distinct segments or subcategories. While these could be cut multiple ways, a typical set of segments would be as follows:

- *Physical*: Tangible objects (What), mechanical processes (How), physical or temporal locations (Where), physical events (When); also align to ***rule-based*** skills (Who) and decisions (Why)

- *Virtual*: Intangible objects such as data (What), software processes (How), logical locations (Where), data-events (When); also align to ***analytic*** skills (Who) and decisions (Why)

- *Relational*: Links to people (What), manual processes (How), social/relational locations (Where), human events (When); also align to ***heuristic*** skills (Who) and decisions (Why)

- *Aspirational*: Principles and values (What), value-webs and dependencies (Where), business-rules (When); also align with ***principle-based*** skills (Who) and decisions (Why)

- *Abstract*: Additional uncategorized segments such as financial (What, How), energy (What), time, etc.

Relationships or "composites" may exist in columns between items in the same segment, or in different segments. We link composites across other columns to create "incomplete" design-patterns, or to complete the composite across all columns for final implementation. This balance between incompletion and completion enables architectural redesign, anchoring trails of relationship between items or layers, to resolve business-concerns such as strategic analysis, failure-impact analysis, and complex pain-points.

This is where we come back to service-oriented architecture and the service-oriented enterprise, because the layering of services – particularly the management-services – maps well onto the layering of that framework, and services themselves are ready-made design-composites that already straddle at least two of the framework columns, *function* and *capability*, and often map easily onto others such as *event* and *asset*. The two columns that don't map so easily are *location* – which is usually an issue around implementation rather than at design-time – and *decision*. Yet the latter is where the pervasive-services come back into the picture, because their role is entirely around the "why" of the enterprise.

So in turn we need to review each of the enterprise pervasive-services in terms of each of the segments of the framework or each of the tetradian dimensions – physical, conceptual, relational, aspirational – since it comes to much the same in practice. For example, consider the pervasive-services that focus on security. The basic assumption, especially in an IT context, would be that it's essentially about the "need to know" – the conceptual dimension. In the machine-metaphor for the enterprise, we might also acknowledge a "need to use" – the physical dimension. Yet that's still only the start: in the living-organism metaphor, we learn to recognize that security becomes "viable" only when we include *all* the tetradian dimensions:

- *Physical*: Need to *use*, need to have access

- *Conceptual*: Need to *know*, need to learn

- *Relational*: Need to *connect*, to relate, interact, or talk with others

- *Aspirational*: Need to *belong*, to share common vision and values

In each dimension, there are consequences of allowing security to be too open. The catch is that those consequences may be felt only in what would otherwise appear to be unconnected aspects of the security context. In the case of email, for example, lax attitudes to relational-security concerns such as rampant forwarding and "for-your-information" copies have a huge cost not just in people's time dealing with email-glut – "too much information!" – but also in disk-storage, bandwidth, and similar physical-dimension themes. It's not a "need to know" issue, but it does need to be understood in the same kind of terms: it's an *overall security* issue that needs to be resolved through appropriate pervasive-services – in this case, education to shift the culture around the overuse of email. And often those cultural issues may echo back and forth into other dimensions: in that example, the real driver might be a climate of fear, with everyone trying to spread responsibility for difficult decisions as far around the enterprise as possible. Pervasive themes are literally pervasive: they impact everywhere in the enterprise, and often in unexpected ways.

Yet there are also consequences to setting security too tight in any dimension – and again, the real impacts may become apparent only in other dimensions. For example, if we shut people off from information that they believe they need for their work, they not only make poorer decisions, but they also lose their sense of belonging to the enterprise – which is likely to have serious impacts on commitment and morale and other aspirational-dimension themes. If we become too obsessed about physical security, such as an overdominant health-and-safety focus, we end up creating a context in which people not only can't do their work (physical-dimension) but also can't learn the requisite skills (conceptual-dimension and aspirational-dimension) and may well become *more* at risk because they don't understand the dangers, inventing unsafe workarounds just to get things done.

So service-completeness applies not just to patterns for design and reuse, but to the broader architectural assessment as well. The recursive approach we've used earlier also inherently acts as a gap-analysis to identify and highlight potential holes in the viability of service-designs and service-structures, and in the enterprise as a whole. And as we move now from principles to practice, we'll start to see how all of these concerns would apply in the real world of the service-oriented enterprise.

# Into Practice

- In what ways would you apply the $R^5$ principles – rotation, reciprocation, resonance, recursion, and reflexion – in architecture-assessment for your own enterprise? Given that some of these concepts may seem alien to "business as usual" thinking, how would you express to others what these tools will show you about the enterprise and its services?

- In what ways does the perspective shift when you replace the term "nonfunctional requirements" with "qualitative requirements"? In what ways do the priorities for solution-designs shift as you do so? For example, do qualitative concerns start to seem more important than before? If so, what could you do to respond to those changed priorities?

- What are the interdependencies between systems in your own enterprise? How would you map the interactions across those links, at each level and within and between each silo in the enterprise? By what means could you use the "service" paradigm to identify and simplify those interfaces?

- What patterns do you identify in your existing system designs and system implementations? In what ways do such patterns enable repurpose and reuse? How do you balance "completion" and "incompletion" – especially in service-design and service-implementation?

- Your existing security-models and security-management for the enterprise will certainly cover the "need to know," and probably the "need to use," but to what extent do they also address the "need to relate" and "need to belong"? What happens to your perception of security overall when you add those extra dimensions to the security picture? What – if anything – can you see that would need to change when you *do* include those dimensions?

# Summary

In this chapter, we were reminded that no service exists in isolation. It exists to serve; it has its own specific nature and properties, and each service has links and dependencies with other services. A "systems" perspective helps in making sense of the complexity of all these concerns, by describing patterns of interrelationships that are known to work in practice. These relationships also clarify options for service repurpose and reuse, via a concept of "completeness" as a guide for service design and implementation.

In the next part of this book, we'll start to use all of these patterns and principles in real-world practice.

# PART III

# Practice – An Overview

The service-oriented enterprise is composed of a myriad of other services at many different scales. As shown in Figure P3-1, we can describe each of these as belonging to one of four categories: delivery, management, coordination, and pervasive quality.

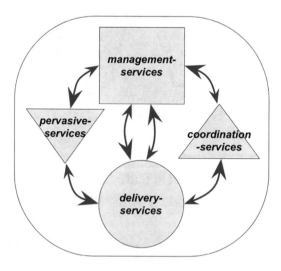

**Figure P3-1.** *Four categories of services*

But in itself, this doesn't tell us much about how the services interrelate with each other in practice, and it also doesn't tell us much about how to describe that real-world practice. For those, our best tactic would be to merge that fourfold service-structure with another five-phase approach to modeling and mapping the architecture of the enterprise, as shown in Figure P3-2.

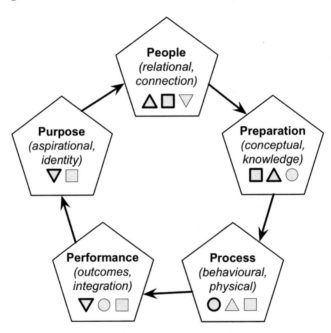

**Figure P3-2.**  *Four categories, five phases*

---

This methodology is described in more depth in the book *Real Enterprise Architecture: Beyond IT to the Whole Enterprise* – see Appendix B, "Resources."

---

So this Practice part is split into five chapters, each describing aspects of service-architecture and the service-oriented enterprise in terms of the respective phase:

- *Purpose*: An emphasis on pervasive-services – "What purpose does the enterprise serve? Whom does it serve?" – see Chapter 10, "Practice – Service Purpose"

- *People*: An emphasis on management-services – "How do services relate with each other?" – see Chapter 11, "Practice – Services and Functions"

- *Preparation*: An emphasis on coordination-services – "What do services know and need to know?" – see Chapter 12, "Practice – The Knowledge of Services"

- *Process*: An emphasis on delivery-services – "What does each service do? How does it do it? How do we coordinate services to get real work done?" – see Chapter 13, "Practice – Services in Action"

- *Performance*: An emphasis again on pervasive-services – "What have we done? How can we improve what we do?" – see Chapter 14, "Practice – Optimizing Services"

Although this cannot cover every possible aspect of service architecture, of course, it should provide enough of a start to put the principles into real practice within the architecture of your own present enterprise.

# CHAPTER 10

# Practice – Service Purpose

To the service-oriented enterprise, the organization itself is a service within the broader shared-enterprise. Yet if it's a service, *whom* does it serve? What *is* the service? What is the *purpose* of the enterprise? Such questions barely matter in the machine-metaphor: after all, it's just a machine... But in the organism-metaphor, those questions go right to the core of the enterprise: the answers to those questions are the *reasons* for its existence.

## Practice Themes: Enterprise As a Service

- Whom does your enterprise serve?

- What purpose does it serve?

- In what ways does it serve?

---

In commercial organizations especially, it's easy to fall prey to cynicism here: "we exist to make the shareholders rich...." That kind of feeling is understandably endemic wherever the Taylorist machine-metaphor dominates, but in the organism-metaphor, it's essential to break free from the cynicism, and instead really explore what it is that brings the enterprise alive.

© Tom Graves 2023
T. Graves, *The Service-Oriented Enterprise*, https://doi.org/10.1007/978-1-4842-9189-4_10

What role does it play in "the wider scheme of things"? If it's a commercial enterprise, ignore the shareholders for a moment – to be blunt, their real business function is merely that of service-providers, for one specific type of resource that the enterprise will need – and concentrate instead on the value-webs in which the enterprise participates. Who are the "customers" here, and in which parts of the value-web? A focus there will give you a clearer set of answers as to whom and for what the enterprise truly exists to serve.

In practice, it may take several iterations through those questions before arriving at answers that seem genuinely meaningful across the enterprise. A classic cue is that an authentic answer will have a kind of emotive resonance, a sense of "rightness" about it – though again, don't expect to arrive at it on the very first try.

If you're using a purpose-built architecture toolset, place the answers as entities in the "Universals" section of the architecture framework (see the section "Service Completeness" in Chapter 9, "Principles – Properties and Patterns"). In any case, document the results for later review.

# Practice Themes: Stakeholders

- Extending "whom does the enterprise serve," who are the stakeholders in the enterprise?

- What are the aims, needs, and purpose for each of these stakeholders?

- What are the common factors between each of these stakeholders? What is the shared "guiding star" that links all of the stakeholders together?

The distinction here is between the "value-chain" and the "value-web." The conventional notion about business value is that there's a single chain of "added value" between the customer and the profit. That is, as usual, a very machine-like way of looking at the issues. In reality, those issues are a great deal more complex, because the customers – like the shareholders, for that matter – are just one group among many who have an active "stake" in the well-being of the enterprise. To take a classic supply-chain view, the stakeholders would include everyone from the supplier's supplier to the customer's customer, and to those we would need to add all the service-providers, and everyone employed in the enterprise, either directly or indirectly; all the families of those people; everyone living in the vicinity of the enterprise workplaces; local governments and legislative or regulatory bodies; and the list goes on and on. To make sense of that vast inventory of conflicting interests, look for a common "guiding star" that links them all: that in turn will give you a clearer pointer to the questions about whom and how the enterprise serves.

# Practice Themes: Stakeholder Imbalance

- Are any specific stakeholders "privileged" above all others?

- If so, who? What imbalances would this cause in the ways the enterprise can serve?

- What could you do in your architecture to redress any such imbalances?

In many contexts, even to ask such questions, let alone act on them, may well seem fraught and politically loaded, to say the least…

But while you're unlikely to have much authority to make changes here, as an architect you *do* have the authority – and responsibility – to identify the impacts of such imbalances and at least suggest what could be done, in terms of enterprise *structure*, to ameliorate those impacts. If any stakeholder has a role that's little better than a parasite, in terms of the organism-metaphor, then as an enterprise-architect it's your *duty* to say so, because that one parasite could well kill the whole enterprise, to everyone's loss – including that of the parasite.

So while these questions may seem simple at first, they do go right to the core of the enterprise. Not trivial at all…

As before, document the answers in the "Universals" section of the framework, and perhaps also use them to review the results from the previous questions.

# Practice Themes: Vision and Values

- What values do each of the stakeholders bring to that shared common purpose?

- What commonalities and conflicts exist between all these different values?

- What values does the enterprise need so as to fulfill its part in that shared purpose?

- What values does the enterprise *actually* express – perhaps as indicated by POSIWID?

- What impacts do any value-mismatches have on the effectiveness of the enterprise in moving toward its espoused aims?

- What would need to be done to ameliorate those impacts? What would need to be done to bring the current actual values in line with those needed?

---

Once again, as an enterprise architect, you may not have the authority to do anything directly about any value-issues. But you *do* have the authority and ability to identify their impacts, and perhaps describe to others what could be done in structural terms to address them.

---

Use value mapping and requirements-modeling techniques to identify enterprise values and their commonalities and conflicts. Document the results in the "Universals" part of the framework.

Techniques such as VPEC-T, SCORE, and even classic SWOT analysis will be helpful in identifying the impacts of any value-conflicts.

# Practice Themes: Policies and Constraints

- What policies will need to apply throughout the enterprise in order to support the vision and espoused values?

- What laws, regulations, standards, policies, and other external constraints will apply to the enterprise from the social and business milieu within which it exists and operates?

Again, requirements-modeling and techniques such as VPEC-T and SCORE will be useful to map these policies and constraints, and the cross-dependencies and conflicts between them.

---

Another good place to start would be to look for the laws, regulations, and standards that apply throughout your industry: banking, for example, is all but drowning in regulations that no-one in the industry can ignore. But then look in more detail at how these regulations and standards apply in *your* organization: there are often subtle nuances there that can be crucially important to the way your organization works. Challenging, yes – but often fascinating, too.

---

Document the results as per the applicable architecture principles and practices; for example, if you're using a Zachman-style framework, these would typically go into row 1, row 2, or even row 3 of the "why" or "reasons" column. Cross-link each of these references back to the appropriate items in the row 0 vision and values.

# The Structure of Purpose

The vision, values, principles, and constraints form the ultimate anchors for the pervasive-services, and in turn also for the trails of performance metrics to be tracked via the management-services.

One common tool for modeling the relationships between these factors is the Business Motivation Model (BMM), developed by the Business Rules Group and now maintained as a formal standard by the Object Management Group (OMG). In our experience, though, it does have a few serious flaws – particularly in its handling of the "vision" layer. For strategy with broader scope, we would usually supplement the BMM with an additional layering of vision, role, mission, and goal:

- *Vision*: A short statement describing a desired "world" or world-condition that engages and encompasses the common interests of all its stakeholders; always greater in scope than the organization itself

- *Role*: A description of what the organization will do, and will not do, in support of the aims of the vision's "world"

- *Mission*: A description of a capability to support the role, which the organization will create, maintain, and, eventually, dismantle as appropriate

- *Goal*: A description of a "project" or equivalent, in support of a mission, with specific deliverables, specific requirements for resources, and a specific target completion-date

Ultimately, for every activity in the organization and the broader enterprise, we should be able to identify an audit-trail of its parent goal, mission, and role, all the way back up to the enterprise vision, as shown in Figure 10-1.

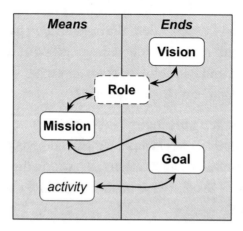

***Figure 10-1.*** *Layering of ends and means: vision, role, mission, goal*

If we view the whole organization as a single delivery-service, what it serves is the shared vision of the broader enterprise. What it does as a service is deliver its role, in conjunction with the role-services delivered by all the other stakeholders. The top-level management is contained within that single top-level delivery-service; the vision is the anchor for the enterprise pervasive-services; and the role acts as an identifier for the inter-enterprise coordination-services.

Each value-chain in the enterprise – in practice, there may be many of them – is served by an ongoing mission, which itself is a delivery-service on the next layer down in the service-hierarchy. Each of these may be served by many other internal missions, capabilities, within the myriad of subenterprises and sub-subenterprises within the broader enterprise. In turn, each goal is an individual, measurable, finite step with the delivery-processes of a mission.

# Practice Themes: Vision, Role, Mission, Goal

- What is the vision for your enterprise? – the broader "storyworld" which all its stakeholders share, and whose aims they hold in common?

- What role – or roles – does the organization play within that "world" of the broader enterprise? What roles does it *not* play and hence leaves open for exchange with other stakeholders in that "world"?

- What missions are required to support the organization's role(s) within the shared-enterprise? What forms do those missions take within the enterprise? In what ways do those missions change over time?

- What goals are required to support those missions?
  How do you monitor that each goal has been achieved?
  How do you ensure that each goal is "on purpose," all
  the way back to the original vision?

In principle, the enterprise has only one vision, and in principle, it should never change, because if it does, it ceases to be the same enterprise. The role – or roles – may change slowly over time; the missions may change more often, morphing somewhat with each change in technology or business-context or whatever; and goals come and go according to their own timescales. But underlying each of these is the same notion of *service*.

## Practice Themes: Mission and Service

- Whom does each mission serve? How do you identify
  and verify these connections?

- What needs does each mission serve? How do you
  identify and verify these needs?

- What is the content of each mission's transaction? How
  do you identify and verify what this content should be?

- How do you identify and verify that the need has been
  served in each service-transaction?

This leads us to a matter of metrics. As we've seen, these are collected initially at the root transaction-layer and are collated and aggregated as they move upward through the management-services tree. We measure each goal on completion; we measure each mission on a continual basis, at regular intervals and verified through occasional audit.

In a sense, there's nothing new in this, of course: every organization does this already, in their own way. The catch is that many organizations structure everything around tasks, each with an endpoint that we'd describe here as a goal – so it can be quite hard there to track the *continuity* that underpins a mission. As enterprise architects, we need to make sure that those metrics are properly in place.

The other challenge, perhaps particularly with ongoing missions, is to make sure that the monitoring-loop is properly closed with occasional audit, in classic VSM fashion. Organizations often rely on external auditors to do this for them – financial-auditors, for example, or safety-inspectors – but that tends to happen only on wide intervals of a year or more: we may need to find other ways to tighten up the feedback-loop and close the gap.

Those metrics then travel back *down* the hierarchy-tree via the pervasive-services to complete the feedback loops for service-monitoring and service-improvement. But how do we know that we have the right metrics in the first place? To do that, we still need the sense of the enterprise as a single unified service.

## Practice Themes: Mission, Goal, and Metrics

- What metrics do you collect for each goal? For what purpose? In what ways do these help to improve the performance of subsequent goals?

- What metrics do you collect for each mission? At what intervals? What kinds of audit-processes do you need to verify those metrics?

- How are those metrics transformed as they pass up the management-services tree? Into what abstractions and aggregates? What purpose does each transform serve?

- How are those metrics reused in subsequent audit and review, passing back down the pervasive-services trees? How do they help to complete the respective feedback-loops for performance-monitoring?

- How are those metrics reused for service-improvement? How does that reuse align with the business-purpose of each service, and the overall purpose of the enterprise as a service?

If the management-services represent "the brain of the firm," the pervasive-services are its heart or soul – its means for staying "on purpose" in relation to the vision. The enterprise-values form the ultimate anchors for the trees of pervasive-services.

# Practice Themes: Staying on Purpose

- How do the enterprise values support the vision? What values are needed in order to support that vision? And by what means would you identify and address any implicit values that would pull the enterprise away from the vision?

- What pervasive-services are needed to support each required enterprise value? How do the respective pervasive-service trees devolve from each enterprise value?

- By what means do the pervasive-services extend throughout the entire enterprise?

- What combinations of awareness-development, capability-development, and audit are required at each layer and in each context? How do these combinations, and the content of each combination, change in differing contexts?

- By what means would you verify that each instance of a pervasive-service supports its respective parent enterprise-value, all the way up the value tree to the enterprise-vision?

- Viewing the entire enterprise as a single service, what else would you need to do or define to ensure that that service remains "on purpose" in relation to the vision?

These questions may seem abstract at first, but they form the underlying foundation of "enterprise *as* a service" for the service-oriented enterprise.

# Summary

In this chapter, we set out to tackle the first question for any service-architecture: "Whom do we serve?" The answers to that question would identify the overall purpose for the services provided by the organization-as-a-service, and the anchors for the architectures that support that need. In exploring this requirement, we went through several linked sets of questions about stakeholders, policies, vision, role, mission, goal, metrics, and more, leading toward a purpose and its practical implications.

In the next chapter, we'll apply that same process to the structures and relationships of services and business-functions, particularly in the context of the people of the organization and the broader shared-enterprise.

# CHAPTER 11

# Practice – Services and Functions

In mathematical terms, a *function* is something that can create a change in accordance with intent. The same is true in business too, and especially at the upper levels of the organization and enterprise, a "function" is almost synonymous with "service." Business-functions *are* services.

So how do we describe how these functions or services interrelate with each other? The layering of delivery-services – the business-functions – is also a layering of the management-services and their resultant silos, and the various ways in which those delivery-services link together across the silos also describe the layering and interactions of the "run the business" coordination-services. In that sense, functions describe the enterprise itself.

Hence, a Functional Business Model is one of the most valuable tools for architecture of the service-oriented enterprise. Once we have the vision and values clearly described, as the anchors for everything else, the next item we'll need is that function-model.

## The Functional Business Model

A Functional Business Model is a layered list of business functions – a visual summary of what the enterprise does in functional or service terms.

© Tom Graves 2023
T. Graves, *The Service-Oriented Enterprise*, https://doi.org/10.1007/978-1-4842-9189-4_11

So the aim here is to create a model that remains much the same as long as the organization does that kind of work.

---

You'll also hear the term "capability-model" or "capability-map" used in place of the Functional Business Model. There are some key technical differences between the two types of models: in effect, a function is an interface for a service, whereas the capability does the actual work. Also, and importantly, a Functional Business Model does reflect the functional (but not organizational) structure of the organization, whereas a capability-model shouldn't care about that at all. But while we'll focus here on the Functional Business Model, there are enough similarities between the two types that, if you already have a capability model, you can probably use that here instead.

---

In order to remain largely unchanged over time, the content of the model needs to be independent as possible from the current management-structure of the organization itself. So in a sense, we run the usual enterprise-architecture process here: we start with the "to-be" model, the description of the idealized organization in its enterprise context, and then work backward from there to link it to what actually exists in the present day. That in turn will give us the gap-analysis that we'll need for future change toward that "to-be" ideal.

The aim is that the model should summarize the *functions* of the whole organization or enterprise on a single page. Although it would fit best on a larger sheet (A3 or 11x17), it should still be readable on a standard single sheet (A4 or 8½x11). In this form, and at this size, it supports understanding across the enterprise, at a "big picture" level. In effect, it provides a high-level visual anchor for the enterprise's business-architecture.

Remember that an "enterprise" here can be at any scale: any subset or superset of an organization. But when the model works well, it provides an instant overview of the whole enterprise, at whatever scale that may be.

In one case, we saw a copy of the model pinned up on the wall in almost every manager's office. They used it to guide conversations about themes such as end-to-end processes, or any process that crosses boundaries between organizational silos – a process being in effect a choreographed path that links business services together to *do* something that contributes toward the organization's goals.

With a completed function-model, we can allocate functions to *business systems* – clusters of activities that do similar things and share similar data in different areas of the enterprise. This simplifies mapping of applications and systems across the whole of the enterprise. We can also map projects and applications to functions, allowing you to see gaps and overlaps in the system coverage, and identify potential for new projects. And by cross-mapping to activity-based costing, we can map costs to functions, highlighting the targeting of project spend. That's a lot of value from one relatively simple model.

The model is laid out in whatever format best describes the business. It could be laid out as a left-to-right flow from "customer" to "delivery," with supporting activities above and below, as in the first of the examples shown later in this chapter; it could be laid out as an open box or any other layout that feels right and makes sense as a business description. But whatever layout is used, it's typically organized as a visual nested-hierarchy, usually with three or four tiers of functions:

- *Tier 1*: Major categories of business functions – key aspects of what the enterprise as a whole actually *does*.

- *Tier 2*: Clusters of related activities – the major support-missions for the tier-1 functions

- *Tier 3*: "Activities" or clusters of related tasks – typically the emphasis of a team's or a person's work.

- *Tier 4*: The individual tasks within business processes – the actual delivery-processes

The tier-4 functions are usually not shown on the diagram, for lack of space, but instead would be listed within a supporting text document. Although there is real value to be gained from gathering the full information at every tier, the cost of doing so rises with the level of detail. The first three tiers are probably essential for any enterprise-modeling exercise, but it's likely that tier-4 information may be worth gathering in depth only when an appropriate project touches the respective area of the enterprise.

# Creating a Function Model

A few key points need to be kept in mind throughout the process of creating a function-model:

- The model needs to be independent of the current organizational structure or business units – for example, an org-chart is in effect an *overlay* on the function model.

- The model needs to be independent of any existing applications – because those are likely to change in the future.

- Each function or activity in effect delivers a service.

To identify candidate functions and activities, trawl through existing documents such as org-charts, strategies, plans, and annual reports, and also intranet sites and the like. Look for the following:

- *Org-chart entries*: Each role implies one or more business functions – though they may overlap, or be repeated in multiple locations, or aggregate several distinct functions.

- *References to projects*: Each is likely to imply a new or upgraded capability, which again implies a function.

- *References to phone-lines, workspaces, or other contact-points*: These imply business-functions behind the points of contact.

---

It's also a good idea to build a network of business acquaintances to help you fill in any gaps. One of my standard tactics is to sit in whatever café is used by staff to get their morning coffee, with a cluster of interesting-looking diagrams casually laid out on the table as if working on them, and then use the diagrams as conversation-starters. But whichever way you do it, such conversations matter here: create them in any way you can.

---

Another source of pointers to functions is the business data. If an enterprise data-model is available, trawl through that, looking for the implied functions that would create, read, aggregate, update, or delete the information-items.

Every business function *does* something, so each function-label on the model should begin with or include a verb. For the tier-1 and tier-2 functions, it would be acceptable to use abstract verbs such as "provide" or "manage," but wherever practicable, and for tier-3 or tier-4 especially, it's advisable to use more specific, descriptive verbs such as "receive," "assess," "monitor," and so on.

# Practice Themes: Tier-1 Functions

- What are the major categories of business functions?

- How do these functions relate with each other, in terms of service-categories and service-layering?

***Figure 11-1.*** *Functions: tier-1 example*

As shown in Figure 11-1, aim to define some 6–12 tier-1 functions. These will usually be obvious in the structure of the enterprise: for example, every organization will have a set of "business support" functions such as HR and finance, a set of contact-points for customers and other stakeholders, a layer for strategy and management, and a set of core business-processes.

---

One common split is on divisional boundaries, but beware of anchoring the model too tightly to the current organizational-structure of the enterprise, because that could well change next week. Instead, aim to make your categories reflect key aspects of what the business actually *does*.

Some industries already have their own generic function-models, such as eTOM for telcos and SCOR for supply-chain and logistics. They'll need adaptation to the specific context of the enterprise, even within the respective industry, but they're useful as guidelines in any case.

## Practice Themes: Tier-2 Functions

For each tier-1 category

- What are the main clusters of related activities that occur within this category?

- How do these functions relate with each other, in terms of service-categories and service-layering?

As shown in Figure 11-2, expect to identify around 40–50 of these in total. They can sometimes be found from job-titles: a truck driver, for example, or a warehouse manager, who each do a range of related business activities and tasks. The org-chart will also give some pointers on this, though again take care not to tie the list too tightly to anything that's likely to change.

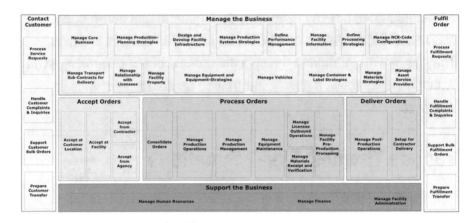

***Figure 11-2.***  *Functions: tier-2 example*

Functions at tier-2 can be harder to identify than those at tier-3 and below; the latter can be detected readily via a trawl through documents and the like. To derive tier-2 functions, look for natural clusterings of tier-3 functions; often, these will be implied by higher-level entries in the org-chart, or by groupings of functions that reappear together in different geographical locations.

---

You're likely to go through several iterations while you're building this part of the model, often with a lot of refactoring and the like going on during the development process. The tier-1 model will be basically the same for every industry, and is unlikely to change much at all, whereas the tier-3 functions are often relatively easy to identify, and themselves won't change as such. But getting the tier-2 layer right is often a lot harder; it's usually *sort of* the same across a given industry, but there are often subtle differences in what each organization does in that industry that can make this stage a lot harder; telecoms and media companies might base their tier-2 model on the eTOM/SID or Frameworx standards, for example, but almost every company in the industry does the work a different way, with different combinations of the various elements for telecoms, the Internet, media, and the like.

Just to make it even more fun, small but important business-functions can pop out of the woodwork in unexpected places; for example, we'd forgotten about the role of the locksmith in a public logistics organization that we were modeling, and adding that one function forced us to change the tier-2 structure all over again. So don't be surprised if you find this part of the modeling to be a lot harder than it might have seemed at the start; it's not your fault that it happens, and, yes, it happens a lot.

---

# Practice Themes: Tier-3 Functions

For each tier-2 cluster of related activities

- What are the main "activities" or clusters of related tasks?

- How do these functions relate with each other, in terms of service-categories and service-layering?

Tier-3 "activities" typically represent the main emphasis of a single person's work. As shown in simplified form in Figure 11-3, aim to identify 200–300 of these – perhaps less in a smaller organization, but not more, in case the model becomes too cluttered to make sense.

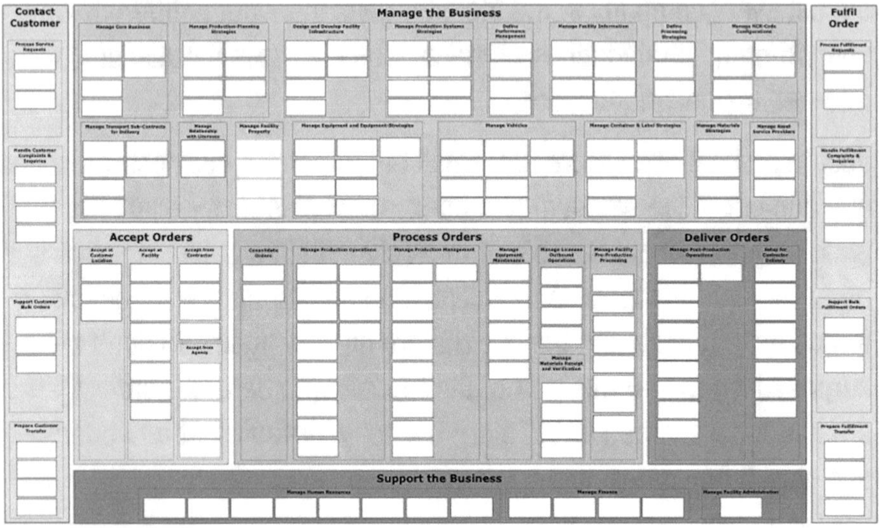

*Figure 11-3.* *Functions: tier-3 example*

A warning: Human nature being what it is, *every* manager will want you to list every one of their business functions on the diagram. You'll need to apply some fairly strong negotiating skills to get the balance right across the whole organization, because there'll never be enough space to list *everything*! As a guide to negotiation, set yourself a strict limit of 250 or so tier-3 functions for the whole enterprise.

All of the functions they describe will be valid, of course, but most will be tier-4 "tasks" which can be listed in the supporting document. What you're after here is the small handful of – to them – higher-level tier-3 functions that summarize their work in relation to everyone else: probably no more than half a dozen functions each, in practice.

Do remember, though, to document any tier-4 functions you come across; they'll be important for end-to-end process-design and information-mapping at later stages in the enterprise-architecture.

# Practice Themes: Tier-4 Functions

For each tier-3 activity

- What are the tasks within the activity?

- How do these functions relate with each other, in terms of service-categories and service-layering?

Unlike the other tiers, which are usually rather more abstract collations or aggregations of business-functions, tier-4 "tasks" will either be or be close to actual tangible work. Since they don't have to be squeezed onto the diagram, there can be any number of these; document them in any way that seems appropriate to the business need.

---

Often, the easiest way to find these tier-4 tasks is to look through process-catalogues or service-catalogues; by definition, each of the elements in those catalogues will imply some kind of task that's being done. Another approach would be to use the tier-3 model as a catalogue for clusters of work, and then just wander around the organization asking how each of these chunks is actually done.

Trying to create and maintain a perfectly complete tier-4 is probably impossible and would almost certainly be overkill anyway. Yet the reason why it may be worth doing at least *some* development on this layer is that it can help other teams do *their* work, on other themes such as activity-based costing and the like. Those themes themselves won't be part of an architect's responsibility, of course, but the architect does come into the picture there in creating the underlying functional-models and suchlike that those themes would use.

---

# Verifying a Function Model

As the model is developed, it needs to be verified for completeness. The simplest way to do this is to think of each function as a service, with each component intimately interlinked with and dependent on all of the other services within the enterprise and (certainly at tier-3 and above) containing other subsidiary services which it coordinates to deliver its overall "product" – whatever that may be. In effect, the whole enterprise delivers one or more services to its clients, and in turn "consumes" services from other entities such as suppliers, partners, government, and other stakeholders.

To verify "completeness" in a viable-services sense, the essential test is that each of the Viable System Model "systems" is present in some form or another: either "contained" within the respective service or provided via a link from some other service. In addition to routine audit in the specific terms for that service, it's also advisable to verify that quality-management of some kind is applied consistently throughout the enterprise, as a mandatory pervasive-service for every context. The checklist that follows addresses all of these concerns, but in practice is only the minimum check that should be applied; add further context-specific tests to the list as appropriate.

## Practice Themes: Verifying a Function Model

Apply the following checklist to each function, and at each tier:

- *Policy*: What is the service's *purpose*? Who or what defines *policy*?

- *Strategy*: What is the current *strategy*? Outside *relationships*? Who defines this?

- *Manage*: How are the service's *tasks defined, managed,* and *monitored*?

- *Verify*: What random checks or *audits* are used to *verify* performance?

- *Coordinate*: How is the service *coordinated* with other services?

- *Tasks*: What does the service *do*? How does it do it? How does it support its "downline" services (if any)?

- *Exceptions*: How does the service identify and resolve any *runtime exceptions*?

- *Quality*: What *corrective-action* does the service undertake for *causes* of issues?

- *Track*: How does the service *track* and manage *quality-issues* and other issues?

- *Improve*: How does the service manage *improvement* of its *processes*?

Each of these checklist-items should reference support-services that this function "consumes," either from other functions or from subsidiary functions and tasks within itself. Every function throughout our function-model must connect *somehow* with at least one support-service that satisfies each of the needs on that checklist, and in principle, each of these support-services must exist *somewhere*; otherwise, the organization would be unable to operate.

---

Or unable to operate *well*, at any rate: hence the notion of a "viable service." A key part of "to-be" functional design is to identify support-relationships for services that the function does not yet contain within itself. Serious viability problems can occur if those support-links are either missing or poorly maintained – the absence of explicit support for corrective-action and quality-management being classic examples that I've seen in all too many business-environments.

---

Document any identified gaps, and work with business-planning teams and suchlike to resolve these gaps wherever practicable.

In many cases, the required support-services or links will in fact exist, but are not recognized as such; they may be implied in what is actually done in practice, but no explicit formal procedures exist to call for them. In others, the links might be subsumed under a generic task-heading of "responsibilities of line-management" or suchlike – but there may be no explicit means to ensure that the work required within the respective-service interrelationship is actually done.

And in some cases, the links may be erratic, or entirely absent, often with results whose symptoms are all too evident, but whose cause is not. High-pressure production environments, for example, are notorious for losing track of any future-focused business-purpose or failing to understand the crucial quality-management distinction between "correction" ("fix it up to get the job out of the door") and "corrective action" ("make sure it doesn't happen again"). All of these concerns – most often from inadequate integration of pervasive-services – need to be resolved before the enterprise can become fully viable, and fully alive.

# Function Model Examples

Two examples of completed function-models follow.

---

A quick note: Both of these example-models would usually be presented in a format at least three or four times larger than shown here; hence, much of the text will probably be too small to read at this scale. Yet the detail doesn't really matter here; the main aim here is just to show what the tier-structure looks like in a typical function-model, and how the overall structure can be changed to suit different business needs.

---

The first example, shown in Figure 11-4, is described as for a plastics-factory – though actually adapted from the function-model for one division of an organization in another industry, de-identified and recaptioned to preserve commercial confidentiality. This shows the relatively simple case of an enterprise with a single straight-through value-chain, from customer-order – in most cases received via another division of the organization, hence only minimally addressed here – through to transfer to fulfillment-processes, which were again handled by another division.

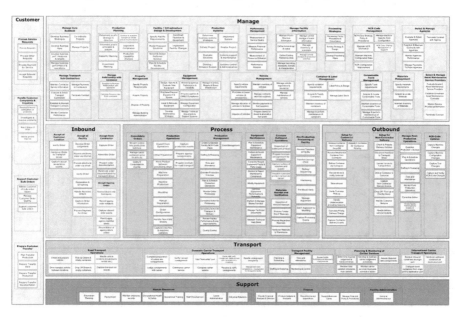

***Figure 11-4.*** *Functions: manufacturing division of (fictional) plastics firm*

The organization had several distributed worksites; hence, inter-site transport was an important factor. The zone shown above the main value-chain provides the policy and strategy management-services and, to some extent, the high-level parts of the pervasive-services; the zone below the "transport" function shows typical support-services provided by central management.

The second example, shown in Figure 11-5, is adapted from an early version of a model developed for a *state-government department* in the social-services sector. This is considerably more complex than the previous example, because it has separate value-streams for each of its five distinct "services to citizens," plus an additional value-stream for its formal relations with government and its many other societal stakeholders.

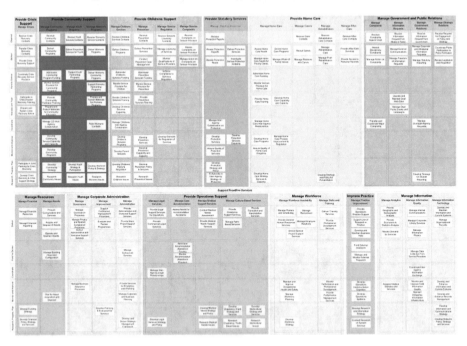

*Figure 11-5.* *Functions: government department in the social-services sector*

All value-streams share many of the same support-services, which makes it inappropriate to use a simple layout of straight-through value-chains, as in the previous example. Instead, a two-tier Viable System Model layout is used, with the main delivery-services shown above as one of the tiers and the support-services shown below as the other.

The same vertical axis is used in both tiers, other than that the "contact" (customer) row is not used in the second tier, because the customer-facing delivery-services are implicitly the "customers" for these support-services. The categories in the vertical axis are as follows:

- *Channel*: Delivery-services (customer-facing only)

- *Deliver*: Delivery-services

- *Fund to deliver*: Delivery-services

- *Educate and train*: Delivery-services

- *Coordinate*: "Direction" management-services, "run the business" coordination-services

- *Monitor and improve*: Pervasive services, "change the business" coordination-services

- *Research, prepare, plan*: "Policy" and "strategy" management-services, "develop the business" coordination-services

Some of the apparent gaps are intentional – for example, some value-streams do not deliver community-education services, and others do not provide internal training. Other gaps, though, are genuine, indicating potential or actual problems for the enterprise.

# Summary

In this chapter, we explored how to map out service-relationships, dependencies, and hierarchies across the enterprise. With the purpose identified, the next architecture requirement is the definition of the services needed to implement it. In doing so, we first need to map how these services would interrelate with each other – particularly the people-aspects of the enterprise. One proven tactic is to create a Functional Business Model as a base-map for subsequent explorations; we worked step by step through how to do this, ending with two real-world worked-examples.

In the next chapter, we'll review the information-flows that need to pass between services in order to create, support, and maintain the overall viability of the enterprise.

# CHAPTER 12

# Practice – The Knowledge of Services

Services exchange information; services *are* information. Their structure and design determine the information that needs to flow around the entire enterprise, so that it can deliver its service, its role within its shared business-context.

---

A quick note: There's a lot to cover in this chapter, and yes, on first read, some of it might perhaps seem "too much theory" or the like. But it's actually all about *practice*: specifically, about making sure that everything connects up properly, that all gaps and overlaps can be found, and that the links that verify alignment to value and governance are all properly in place. It's true that there's a lot of work here for enterprise-architects, but it's probably the only way to ensure that our organizations won't get plagued with odd and seemingly "inexplicable" miscommunications and failures. So it's work that's definitely worth doing, and that we *do* need to know how to do – hence the content of this chapter.

---

© Tom Graves 2023
T. Graves, *The Service-Oriented Enterprise*, https://doi.org/10.1007/978-1-4842-9189-4_12

Developing the Function Model – as a model of the enterprise in terms of its business functions – is a key step in establishing a service-oriented view of enterprise information, because we can use it as a base on which to build a variety of overlays that have high value in the architecture of the enterprise. One of these overlays is the Business Systems Model: this is worth exploring in depth here, with a detailed set of diagrams at the end of the explanation to show how it all works.

The purpose of the model is to identify groups of activities that perform the same kinds of functions and are likely to share the same kinds of information, and hence should be supported by similar information-systems. One of the practical aims of this is to ensure that the computer-systems that are developed or purchased to manage this information do not overlap in functionality or in the information that they store.

Even though this is primarily about information-management, the term "systems" here is more in the Viable System Model sense, rather than just IT-systems. Remember that much of the core information of an enterprise is word-of-mouth, or individual or collective memory, or built into work-instructions for machines and the like. IT plays an important part in all of this, of course, but it's by no means the only part. Whenever we look at "information systems," remember also to think of information in its broadest, generic terms – not just the subset of information that's in computer networks and databases.

The simplest way to build this Business Systems Model is by using color-coding for the tier-3 activities on the Function Model. Each color-code represents a different "business system" or clustering of related activities. For example, we could split some of the business-systems by service-category-type:

- Is the information about "develop the business," "change the business," or "run the business"?

- Is it about a specific category of delivery-service?

- Is it about funding, people-management, or customer-relationships?

And so on, and so on. The most appropriate split will depend on the nature of the enterprise – the service delivered by the organization as a whole, within its shared enterprise context. Hence, there are no straightforward guidelines; but in practice, typically aim to identify some 10–20 distinct shared areas of information. The resultant set of models would consist of the color-coded Function-Model diagram and a set of detailed diagrams, for each of the business systems, together with an appropriate textual description.

# Practice Themes: Identifying Business Systems

- Which tier-3 activities, whether in the same part or different parts of the enterprise, have similar functions and share much the same information?

- What IT-systems or other information-systems would or – for "to-be" – should these activities use? In IT terms, what applications are or should be used to store and access this information?

- As a cross-check, what existing business-information, information-systems, or applications do *not* seem to be used by any activity on the Function Model? What changes would this suggest to the Function Model itself?

Don't expect only a single business-system to apply throughout all of a tier-2 block, and certainly not at a tier-1 level. For example, imagine a tier-2 block that encapsulates the business-function of a production-line context: although the focus may be on the production itself, it will still connect to other business systems such as staff-rosters, materials-stores, and maintenance that each manage their own distinct types of information and concerns that will be shared by their counterparts in other tier-2 functions.

We then run the whole process backward as a further cross-check. For each business system, we need to review the business activities, to verify the "chunks" of information-functions and the like that would be required to support those business activities. This leads us toward the definition of an Information Systems Model, in which these chunks of functionality and related storage are "information systems" in an abstract sense: they are "logical" in that they don't describe any specific application, for example, but do describe in broad terms what the IT and other applications should do.

We define the information systems at the whole-of-enterprise level, and *without reference to existing applications*. This ensures that, overall, the systems and activities each perform functions that make sense to perform together, that there are no overlaps in functionality, and that all of the required functionality is covered. The resultant Information Systems Model consists of an overview diagram or "context diagram" and a set of more detailed diagrams for each of the "information systems," together with a textual explanation of the content and role of each system.

At the end of this process, each business-system should ideally be aligned with precisely *one* information-system. There would usually be a variety of applications that might draw on and manipulate that information, but preferably a *single* shared datastore in each case. That's certainly the ideal for any "to-be" design, though it may not work out that way in practice – especially not in the "as-is" setup. But what we're really aiming for here is that for each business-system, there will be just *one* "database of record": a *single source of truth*, in the information sense of the term.

So, to give a full example of how all of this works, we could start with that first example Function Model from the previous chapter, as shown in Figure 12-1.

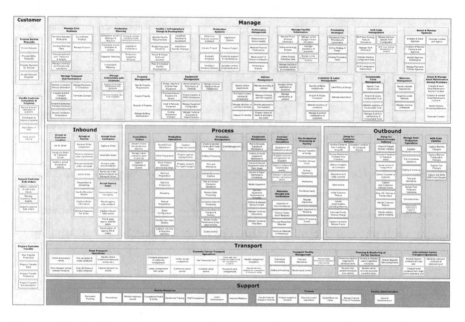

***Figure 12-1.*** *Functions: manufacturing division of (fictional) plastics firm*

We would derive the Business Systems Model from that function-model, using the methods described earlier, and then color-code them on the model, as shown in Figure 12-2.

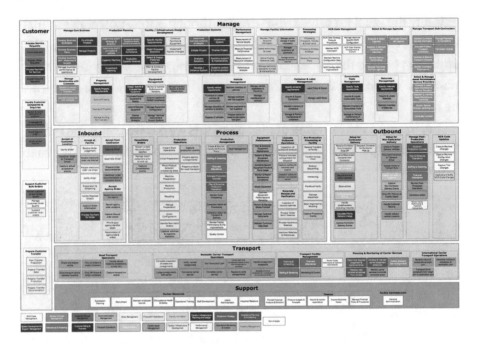

***Figure 12-2.*** *Business-systems color-coded onto the function-model*

We would then build a more detail-level model for each business-system, with its connections to other color-coded business-systems, as shown in Figure 12-3.

Business System Model – Production Operations (Main Facility)

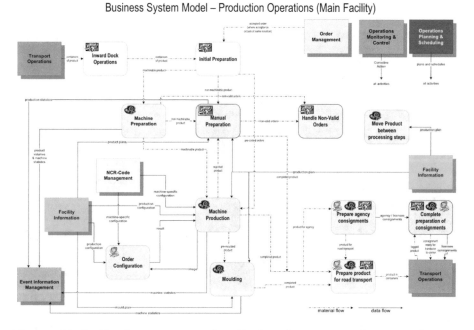

***Figure 12-3.*** *Business-system detail, showing connections to other business-systems*

(The icons in that diagram – the computer screen, the gears, and the assembly-line – respectively represent an IT-based process, a machine-based process, or a people-based process. Where two or more icons are shown on the same function, it means that the function uses a combination of those types of methods.)

And finally, we derive the set of Information Systems Models that underpin the respective business-systems, as shown in Figure 12-4.

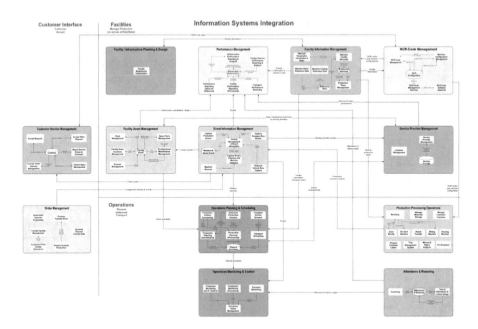

**Figure 12-4.** *Information systems derived from the business-systems on the function-model*

---

Note that all of these models were originally presented at much larger scale than shown here – hence, the detailed captions may not be fully readable. But that isn't important, because the main point here is simply to show how each type of model is derived in turn from the previous ones in the sequence.

---

As described earlier, each business-system should ideally be aligned with precisely one information system, and each of those information-systems should ideally have just one core information-store – its "single-source-of-truth." In the next step, we explore how you would identify that core information store and how it should be used.

# Practice Themes: Identifying Single-Source-of-Truth

For each identified business-system and its information-system

- What are the sources for transaction-data and related metadata for this system?

- Who is the "owner" of each part of the overall information-system – the person who is ultimately responsible for the information that it manages and contains?

- Who or what may create, read, update, or delete transaction-records for this system? For what purposes?

- Who or what may collate transaction-records into aggregations or transformations such as counts-of, trends-of, averages-of, and suchlike? For what purposes? Via what transform-processes? Where and in what systems are such transforms maintained? Who or what may create, read, update, or delete these transforms, or the means by which the transforms take place?

- What audit-trails exist for changes and aggregations of transaction-data for this system?

- What services does each information-item provide or support?

- Is there a "single source of truth" for information in this system? If not, what are the consequences of having more than one source of truth?

Reassess the information-systems, the business-systems, and all the way back to the Function Model, in the light of the results of this review.

# The Value of Services

The next step is to use services as a way to map value for the enterprise, in terms of cost, of returns, or whatever. The Function Model provides an index into the activities of the enterprise: by mapping any set of values onto the model, we gain a picture of the enterprise in relation to that type of value.

Typical costing information for this kind of map might include

- Capital expenditure

- Operational expenditure

- Activity-based costing

- Asset valuation

- Investment-valuation

Other options might include financial return – the classic "return on investment." Note, though, that even in a commercial organization, monetary profit may not be the most important value to track here: the most effective core-values to be monitored are those that are linked to enterprise vision, and which are managed via the pervasive-services rather than solely through the financial accounting-systems.

Other cross-maps that are likely to be useful for whole-of-enterprise optimization include

- Activities directly or indirectly affected by projects

- Activities directly or indirectly affected by changes to legislation or regulation

- Activities using specific applications or other assets

- Activities in specific geographies or assigned to specific business units

The value to be gained from these cross-maps depends most on the level of granularity – in other words, how far down you go into the tiers of the Function Model. A cross-map that stops at tier-1 is unlikely to tell you anything that you don't already know, but going all the way down to tier-4 tasks is probably going to be prohibitively expensive in time and effort – assuming you already have consistent task-mapping across the whole enterprise, which itself is too expensive for all but the most bureaucratic of organizations. If you already have the information to hand, do use it; if not, the usual "keep it simple" rule applies!

Our experience is that most trade-offs end up somewhere between tier-2 and tier-3. For valuation-maps, the cost of collecting the information starts to be prohibitive beyond tier-2 unless the accounting-systems are already set up to support it, but the map is useful even at that relatively coarse granularity.

For project cross-maps, though, you really do need to go down to tier-3, to enable the cross-links to the Business Systems Model and Information Systems Model – which are likely to be important, if not essential, in describing the impact of projects across the whole enterprise context. We used these project cross-maps all the time in our architecture-work, to show us which parts of the overall enterprise each project would touch and also to help us identify overlaps between projects and gaps that weren't covered by any change-project in the overall project-portfolio.

# Practice Themes: Function-Model Overlays

- What costing information or other valuations do you have that can be mapped onto the Function Model? What does such a map show you about the relative cost or value of each activity, at each tier of the Function Model?

- Map current or future projects onto the respective activities on the Function Model, and cross-reference this to the costing maps: What does this tell you about relative targeting of project investment vs. activity value? What project overlaps – if any – are highlighted by this cross-map? Which activities are *not* covered by any change-programs?

These cross-maps will usually highlight architecture-or project-issues that need to be addressed. This is especially true in the early stages of a shift toward a service-oriented enterprise, so don't be surprised at this: just tackle the issues as they arise.

---

A warning that some of these cross-maps can be embarrassing in a business sense – even scary, sometimes. In one enterprise, for example, we found that we had half a dozen projects, with a total cost of some 20 million dollars, all tackling one area of business that was worth barely a tenth of that, while the highest-value aspects of the business received no attention at all. As usual, the culprit there was inappropriate IT-centrism – doing IT "solutions" for the sake of it, without awareness of its impact on *overall* performance.

In another case, in a logistics environment, we found that we had three distinct projects, each requiring separate but incompatible RFID radio-tracking infrastructures, each of them demanding to take exclusive control of the same physical space. No-one had previously thought to check. Ouch...

In yet another case, though, an odd gap in coverage pointed to the unexpected merits of a small, unimportant-seeming project that had previously been turned down twice as having no apparent business-case. On its own, it didn't, but the cross-map showed that it would act as the linchpin for half a dozen other major projects, greatly increasing *their* overall value to the enterprise. Once we'd explained that to the executive, the project gained its go-ahead in a hurry.

Embarrassing or not, such matters are important in optimizing the ability of the enterprise to deliver its services. And as enterprise-architects, that's what we're here to do: this is part of how we get good at doing it!

---

One of the main ways we can do this is to use service-architecture concepts as a guide; for each area of impact, what are the delivery-services and the management-services? What coordination between services would be required? What values need to be supported and monitored in each context, via what pervasive-services? Once we establish that as a review-pattern for each of these cross-maps, the service-oriented enterprise tends almost to create itself.

---

Another quick aside here: This kind of per-project mapping could be a huge overhead for the enterprise-architecture team if they try to do it all on their own. A much simpler and more reliable approach is to teach the project-teams to do it themselves, as part of their routine project-setup; the architecture-team then works with the Project Office to cross-map that already-verified data onto a central model as each project comes in, making the task of looking for gaps and overlaps much easier to do.

---

# Verifying Viability

Another use of the Function Model is as a means to verify viability of all services across the enterprise. To do this, we use much the same process and checklist as when verifying the validity of the overall model, but this time it's not just about confirming that the required links exist, but more about validating the viability of each of the links themselves.

The key theme here is that each entity on the Function Model not only represents a service but also, in effect, implies reference to the respective "direction" management-service and other support-services that are needed for governance of that service. We use the viable-services model to tell us which relationships we will need between the service represented by that entity, and the respective "direction" service and other categories and subtypes of services. All of those other services will need to be in place *somewhere*, so that we can link to them and support overall viability for this service and for the enterprise as a whole. Sometimes, the required links are internal to the activity, but often they're not, and that's what we aim to identify here.

# Practice Themes: Viable Relations

For each tier-3 activity

- Who or what provides "policy" management-services for this activity? If it exists, is it internal or external to the activity? If external, is it spread across more than one other activity?

- Who or what provides "strategy" management-services for this activity? If it exists, is it internal or external to the activity? If external, is it spread across more than one other activity?

- Who or what provides "develop the business" coordination-services for this activity? If it exists, is it internal or external to the activity? If external, is it spread across more than one other activity? With what other services does it coordinate these tasks?

- Who or what provides "change the business" coordination-services for this activity? If it exists, is it internal or external to the activity? If external, is it spread across more than one other activity? With what other services does it coordinate these tasks?

- Who or what provides "run the business" coordination-services for this activity? If it exists, is it internal or external to the activity? If external, is it spread across more than one other activity? With what other services does it coordinate these tasks?

- Who or what acts as the "parent" delivery-service for this activity? In what ways does the parent coordinate resources for this and its other "child"-activities? What performance-information needs to be passed to the parent for this purpose? If other information is passed "upward" or "downward" with the parent for other purposes, what information, and for what purposes?

- Who or what acts as the "child" delivery-services – if any – for this activity? In what ways does this activity coordinate resources for its "child"-activities? What performance-information needs to be garnered from the "child"-activities for this purpose? If other information is passed "upward" or "downward" with the children for other purposes, what information, and for what purposes?

- Who or what provides "run the business" coordination-services for the "child" tasks (if any) of this activity? If it exists, is it internal or external to the activity? If external, is it spread across more than one other activity? With what other services does it coordinate these tasks?

- For each enterprise value, who or what provides "develop awareness" pervasive-services for that value in this activity? Who or what provides "develop capability" pervasive-services for that value in this activity? Who or what provides "audit" pervasive-services for that value in this activity? If each exists, is it internal or external to the activity? If external, is it spread across more than one other activity? How do these link back to the core values of the enterprise?

In effect, this also provides the content for a RACI matrix for each activity:

- *Responsible or "accountable"*: The business-owner of the activity (there should be exactly one person – not just a role but a real person – with this assignment for each activity)

- *Assists*: Those who assist the responsible person in the overall work of the activity

- *Consulted*: Those whose opinions may be sought concerning the activity (two-way communication)

- *Informed*: Those who need to be kept up-to-date on changes concerning the activity (one-way communication)

In RACI terms, the links identified in the preceding review point to activities with an "assists"-relationship to the respective activity. In effect, each of these is a stakeholder in the activity – which means that each link will also point to people who will often need to be consulted, or at the least to be informed, about any changes to the activity. So in addition to identifying mutual cross-dependencies, this also creates a map of mutual responsibilities across the entire enterprise.

The next stage is to map the *content* of each of these links, which in turn points to the required *structure* – and hence the appropriate types of implementation for each link.

# Practice Themes: Viable Communications

For each link to and from each tier-3 activity

- What *physical* resources and other items would be transferred across the link? By what means should these items be transferred? What storage-measures, security-measures, and other qualitative concerns should apply to such transfers?

- What information and other *virtual* assets should be exchanged across the link? By what means should these items be exchanged? What storage-measures, security-measures, and other qualitative concerns should apply to each exchange?

- What interpersonal connections and other *relational* issues apply to each link? By what means should these connections be established and maintained? What security-measures and other qualitative concerns should apply to each connection?

- What purpose and other *aspirational* concerns apply to each link? By what means should these concerns be established and verified? What security-measures and other qualitative themes should apply to each of these concerns?

- What other *abstract* concerns such as time, finance, and funding would apply across the link? By what means should these concerns be identified, applied, and verified? What security-measures and other qualitative themes should apply to each of these concerns?

This review provides a model not just of existing structures and services but also of any "missing" capabilities that would need to exist in order to support viability across the enterprise. In that sense, it amplifies our *knowledge* of the enterprise and its services.

All of this is valuable from an IT perspective, because it identifies content and structure for the Information Systems Model, and the IT-systems and applications that would be needed to support it. But we do need to be thinking wider than just IT-style "service-oriented architecture": these are the transactions across the *whole* of the service-oriented enterprise, not just its IT – and we may need to implement those exchanges and transactions in many different ways.

# Summary

In this chapter, we explored how to use the Function Model as a standard reference-platform for a broad range of other concerns and cross-maps. These might include Business-Systems Models, Information Systems Models, information-flows, costings, project-scopes, assets, applications, business risks, and much else besides. Such cross-references between the domains create new options for whole-of-enterprise optimization.

In the next chapter, we'll bring all of this out of the abstract and more toward the real-world, to review how to design and implement the actual services and service-choreography for a service-oriented enterprise.

# CHAPTER 13

# Practice – Services in Action

On their own, services do nothing. To be useful – to contribute to the overall service of the enterprise – they need to be linked to other services in a choreographed sequence of transactions, as a *business process*. So it's here that we turn to the standard process-modeling tools and techniques, in order to describe the runtime relationships between services and the choreography mechanisms that link them together into a business-process.

So let's take a (much-simplified) example of a service to create a new account, as described in the standard BPMN (Business Process Modeling Notation) format.

As shown in Figure 13-1, this identifies and describes the following components:

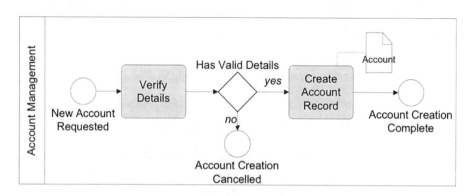

***Figure 13-1.*** *Simplified content of encapsulated service "Create Account"*

© Tom Graves 2023

T. Graves, *The Service-Oriented Enterprise*, https://doi.org/10.1007/978-1-4842-9189-4_13

- The overall service, and responsibility for the service, indicated by the enclosing "swimlane" rectangle and its descriptive label

- The start, end, and exception-end events, represented by circles

- Calls to two child-services, represented by rounded-rectangles

- A decision – part of the internal choreography – represented by a diamond

- An artifact of some kind for the resultant account, represented by a folded-paper symbol

- The sequence of interactions, represented by the connecting lines

---

For this example, don't worry too much about details of the layout or content or suchlike. We could just as well describe it in the form of a UML (Unified Modeling Language) process-diagram, or any other process-modeling notation; the presentation would differ somewhat, of course, but the principles would be much the same. The specific form or representation doesn't much matter here; it's the *principles* we're concerned with – the modeling of service *as* a service.

---

But notice also what is *not* described in that process-model:

- No indication as to *how* the service is implemented, or what form the account-artifact should take

- No indication as to what happens before the start-event or after either of the end-events, or what information or other resources are transferred to or from the service on those events

- No indication of what information and other resources are used within the service

- No indication of what information and other resources are referenced but not consumed within the service

- No indication of what performance-metrics should be provided by the service, or to which other services they should be provided

- No indication of how to verify and maintain quality within the operations and outcomes of the service

Many of those concerns would be addressed in a more detailed model – particularly about any information and other artifacts to be transferred to and from the service. There *is* a definite problem in both BPMN and UML, in that both seem to assume that any resources will always be virtual – hence BPMN's term "data object" for what should really be a generic artifact – and that both at least imply that execution would always be via IT. But in fact, there's no reason to assume an IT-only implementation; the service in that example could just as well be delivered by an entirely manual, paper-based process, or even by a machine-based one in some industrial contexts. The fact that implementation is not predefined in the model is not a mistake, it's a *necessary* requirement for all "logical"-layer modeling.

More relevant here, perhaps, is that there are no assumptions about how the "child" subprocesses are to be implemented. They might indeed be handled by "child" delivery-services; they might instead be in line within this service; the choice doesn't matter much, in principle at least, though there may be practical considerations that could drive the choice one way or the other in different implementations.

More worrying is that there really is no built-in means in either of those modeling-notations to enforce support for those essential performance-metrics. There's also very little acknowledgment of how the choreography and coordination-processes would actually happen. That's a typical consequence of the machine-metaphor, in which choreography is presumed to be a "brain" function from outside of "the machine" itself, but it's an oversight that causes real difficulties when translating a BPMN model even into a form suitable for IT execution, let alone for anything else.

In practice, these things *matter*: we need to be ready for them in designing viable services. Even if the internal service-execution is much the same, a process that needs different performance-metrics or different control-artifacts may well need support from a different service.

# Practice Themes: Process-Choreography – Processes

For each business-process

- Which services link other services together into the choreography of this business-process? Through what mechanisms does that choreography occur? What service-contracts apply to the choreography *as* a service in itself?

- What signals – synchronous, asynchronous, whatever – are in use to ensure that processes happen in the right sequence, at the right time, and in response to the right events? What form do these signals take?

- What mechanisms are used to handle exceptions in the execution of the process? To which services are any exceptions passed, and what types of exceptions in each case? What actions must be taken once the exception is passed?

- What resources are needed for this coordination-service to operate? Via which management-services does it obtain the required resources?

- What performance-metrics does it collate, from individual services within the process-choreography, and from within itself? To what management-services does it pass these performance-metrics?

- What management-services define policy and strategy for this choreography-service?

- What, if any, are the "child"-services for this service?

- Which coordination-services provide "develop the business," "change the business," and "run the business" support for this service?

- Which pervasive-services guide and audit compliance with quality-concerns and other enterprise-values for this service?

# Practice Themes: Process-Choreography – Services

For each service in the business-process

- What interfaces are exposed for choreography-services to discover? Via what mechanisms may the choreography-process discover that interface? Via what mechanisms may the choreography-process identify that the service is available for transactions? Through what mechanisms may a transaction occur? What service-contracts apply to the transactions?

- What mechanisms are used to handle exceptions in the internal execution of the service? Via what mechanisms are any exceptions notified to the connecting choreography-process, and what types of exceptions in each case? What rollback and other actions must be taken by the service once the exception has been passed?

- What resources are needed for this service to operate in different process-choreographies? Via which management-services does it obtain the required resources?

- What performance metrics does the service collate regarding its transactions in service choreographies, from within itself, and from any "child"-services? To what management-services does it pass these performance-metrics?

- What management-services define policy and strategy for the use of this service in process-choreographies?

- Which coordination-services provide "develop the business," "change the business," and "run the business" support for the use of this service in process-choreographies?

- Which pervasive-services guide and audit compliance with quality-concerns and other enterprise-values for when this service is used in process-choreography by "external" services?

This may seem like a lot to assess, but none of it is trivial in its importance. One of the most common architectural problems we see in IT-centric contexts is that while the IT-execution is usually excellent, the handling of anything non-IT will often range from poor to abysmal to nonexistent. Too often, everything non-IT gets shoved into the "too-hard basket," and then promptly forgotten, with disastrous consequences that sooner or later will hit home very hard indeed. Formal service-management processes such as ITIL (IT Infrastructure Library) will help, but tend to be at too high a granularity: they deal with the human side of IT-management, but not so much with the handovers between IT and everything else in the detail of runtime processes – and the latter is where things tend to fall apart. It's that detail that we aim to address in reviews such as those mentioned earlier.

# Breaking Free from IT-Based Assumptions

IT-centrism is probably *the* single greatest problem at present for service-oriented architectures. A service is a service: the choice of mechanism by which it's implemented should always be a secondary concern relative to the structure and role of the service itself. But the seemingly obsessive IT-centrism of the present means that the architecture process often ends up being run backward: we start with some IT-based capability, then look for services to implement with it – and any services that can't be implemented by IT are ignored as "out of scope." This inevitably results in process-gaps that are "invisible" *because* they're not amenable to implementation by IT. In short, it's a guaranteed recipe for disaster – which is exactly what we see in all too many would-be service-architectures.

## Practice Themes: Challenging IT-Centrism

- What tendencies do you see in your own enterprise toward IT-centrism – the implicit assumption not only that every problem has an IT-based solution but that the latest style of IT-based solutions will always be inherently *better* than any other option?

- In what ways is such IT-centrism reflected in the enterprise-architecture, or in the tools, methods, and frameworks used to support it?

- What are the consequences of such IT-centrism? For example, what clashes arise as a result between IT and the rest of the business? And what could you do within the enterprise-architecture to defuse some of these clashes?

The core of the problem is actually a side-effect of IT's own success. It's so well suited to managing all manner of rule-based contexts that it's easy to believe that IT would excel at handling *everything* – which it doesn't. In particular, it is *not* good with true complexity or uniqueness – especially uniqueness at scale. And unfortunately, whether we like it or not, much of the real world *is* complex and *does* include a lot of uniqueness – which means straightaway that almost every rule-based system is at risk of failing in unexpected ways.

In effect, IT-centrism is a kind of last-gasp version of the machine-metaphor, the assumption that the world "ought to be" predictable in the ways that we want and expect, so that everything can be "under control" at all times. Whenever IT-centrism meets the real world, there's always a reflex attempt to force the world to fit the constraints of its rule-based logic, and then complain that the world is somehow being unfair when it doesn't conform to those expectations. The psychology of all this is kind of interesting – but it doesn't help all that much. What *does* help is being clear about what IT is good at, and what it isn't, and using each approach appropriately. There's a kind of gradation here:

- *Rule-based*: No choice or judgment permitted, little to no true skill; real-time or near-real-time only, and strictly causal; may be implemented by machines, IT, or people

- *Analytic*: Some judgment required, with choices among complicated paths, sometimes with delays and disconnects in time, but modeled in terms of cause-effect relationships; usually cannot be implemented by physical machines without IT-based or human support

- *Heuristic*: True skills and judgment always required, to assess contextual patterns with high uncertainties, limited statistical probabilities, complex delays, and unknown or unidentified factors; apparent patterns of cause-effect identified only retrospectively; cannot be implemented by machines or conventional IT-based systems without human support

- *Principle-based*: Very high skill-levels, extreme and inherent uncertainty in real-time or near-real-time; no direct cause-effect patterns identifiable (such as in a "market of one"); can only be implemented by humans

The further we move away from a simple rule-based context, the more expensive the IT becomes, and whenever there's a shift to true complexity, the IT is usually so costly, unreliable, inefficient, or any such that there *must* be a way to hand over to a "manual" version of the process. If there isn't a way to escalate an exception up to a human decision, or some other people-based means to provide the *same* nominal service, that service will eventually fail. It's as simple as that. So we need to design for that from the beginning – *not* just as an afterthought.

---

One of our government clients gave us an example of this, which for them had proved embarrassing in the extreme. Newspaper headlines yet again about apparent failures at the department: a Category One incident must be resolved within a single day, thundered the editorial, yet here were *ten* Category Ones in *one suburb* that still hadn't been closed off in *more than a month*. What's gone wrong *this* time?

Nothing much, in reality. It was indeed true that there were ten distinct reports, and it was also true that they still hadn't been cleared after more than a month. Yet in fact they all related to the same single incident, concerning an unborn child, which had indeed been fully resolved within a matter of a few hours. But they couldn't link the reports together until they had a database record for the child, and they couldn't create that record, because the key-field was date-of-birth – and the child hadn't been born yet. No manual override, hence no way to mark the incident as cleared – and hence a field-day for the first investigative journalist who happened to glance at the statistics published on the department's own website. Oops…

Moral of this story: If you don't want to appear as your local equivalent of bad headlines in the newspaper, make sure that every single one of your services allows some means to do a manual override…

---

Note that this occurs not just with decisions about information but with physical skills too: each new generation of machinery has been created by someone with a high degree of skill pushing the technology beyond its normal limitations.

The same applies to the relational dimension of business. As many banks have discovered the hard way, there are indeed limits as to how many types of transactions that the customers are willing to do only through ATMs and other IT; at some point, they will *need* to talk with a real person, if only to resolve some exception that the IT can't handle – or has created in the first place. Service-oriented architecture is not just about the detail-level IT, but is ultimately about *service* – in every sense of that term.

So we need to extend SOA beyond IT, to the *whole* of the enterprise. Yet we should still aim to use the same core principles as described for IT-based SOA back in Chapter 2, "Basics – Service-Oriented Architecture":

- Loosely coupled

- Contract-based

- Discoverable

- Abstraction and encapsulation

- Reusable and recomposable

- Interchangeable with equivalent services

To illustrate this, we could take an example of services at almost the opposite extreme from IT-SOA, but still recognizable to and relevant for enterprise-architects, namely, a free-form consortium of consultants:

- Each consultant in the consortium presents a *service* – each has specific skills and experience to offer.

- A business-process such as strategy might call on any number of these consultants, in any order: in that sense, the interface would be *loosely coupled*.

- There would need to be some kind of *contract*-relationship, whether formal or informal.

- The consultants and their services would need to be *discoverable*, with identifiable interfaces – if only in the form of email-addresses and the like.

- We know what kind of results we want from the consultants, but how they do that work would be largely up to them: in that sense, there's *abstraction* and *encapsulation*.

- We might use the consultants in almost any order, and in many different tasks and processes; their services are *reusable, recomposable*, and, to some extent, *interchangeable.*

So it all fits: the same architecture principles apply. But what else needs to happen, architecturally speaking, to make this kind of service-oriented consortium a reality? We can use the same review-process as before to explore this service-context, with each usage of the consortium as a business-process in its own right, each with its own choreographed sequence of connections and contextual transactions.

## Practice Themes: Consultancy As a Service

For each business-process that uses the consortium

- Which services link the consortium's services together into the choreography of this business-process? Through what mechanisms does that choreography occur? What service-contracts apply to the choreography as a service in itself?

- What signals – synchronous, asynchronous, whatever – are in use to ensure that the services of the different consultants are called for in the right sequence, at the right time, and in response to the right events? What form do these signals take?

- What mechanisms are used to handle exceptions in the execution of the process? To which services are any exceptions passed, and what types of exceptions in each case? What actions must be taken once the exception is passed?

- What resources are needed for this coordination-service to operate? Via which management-services does it obtain the required resources?

- What performance-metrics does it collate, from individual services within the process-choreography, and from within itself? To what management-services does it pass these performance-metrics?

- What management-services define policy and strategy for this choreography-service?

- What, if any, are the "child" services for this choreography-service?

- Which coordination-services provide "develop the business," "change the business," and "run the business" support for this consortium *as* a service?

- Which pervasive-services guide and audit compliance with quality-concerns and other enterprise-values for the overall services of the consortium?

For each service within the overall business-process – each member of the consortium

- What interfaces are exposed for choreography-services to discover? Via what mechanisms may a choreography-process discover that interface? Via what mechanisms may the choreography-process identify that the service is available for transactions? Through what mechanisms may a transaction occur? What service-contracts apply to the transactions? What forms would those interfaces and transactions take? And what artifacts would be transferred in either direction as part of each transaction?

- What mechanisms are used to handle exceptions in the internal execution of the service? Via what mechanisms are any exceptions notified to the connecting choreography-process, and what types of exceptions in each case? What rollback and other actions must be taken by the service once the exception has been passed?

- What resources are needed for this service to operate in different process-choreographies? Via which management-services does it obtain the required resources?

- What performance-metrics does the service collate regarding its transactions in service-choreographies, from within itself, and from any "child"-services? To what management-services does it pass these performance-metrics?

- What management-services define policy and strategy for the use of this service in the consortium's process-choreography?

- Which coordination-services provide "develop the business," "change the business," and "run the business" support for the use of this service in the consortium's choreographies?

- Which pervasive-services guide and audit compliance with quality-concerns and other enterprise-values for when this service is used in process-choreography by "external" services? What *are* the enterprise vision, values, policies, regulations, and other pervasive themes for the consortium?

At first glance, this may seem a lot more complex than for something like a simple web-service setup. Yet while it's true that the context being managed by the consortium may be quite a bit more difficult to define, with interfaces that tend to be much more free-form in nature, the exact same principles do apply in both cases.

It's not that the consortium is inherently more difficult to design, it's more that IT service-designers tend to leave out half of that list from their analyses, with unfortunate consequences such as those we've seen earlier. Service-oriented architecture can be applied to any context and should apply in the same ways throughout *every* aspect of the service-oriented enterprise.

---

That said, the politics of that shift to a true service-oriented enterprise can be challenging, sometimes in the extreme. It *is* doable: Amazon did it years ago, which eventually led to the creation of Amazon Web Services (AWS) and others of its now-open public-facing services, becoming a huge commercial success. And Ray Anderson's Interface, Inc. – mentioned earlier in this book – did it when they changed over from selling carpet as product to selling the service of covered floors, as did Rolls-Royce Aviation when they changed from selling aircraft-engines to thrust-hours per aircraft.

In each of those cases, though, the change was driven by the CEO, right from the top of the organization – and that does seem to be essential for success. If we don't have that level of support, in unfailing form, the politics can become so hard that we may struggle to succeed. A colleague's painful tales come to mind at this point, about what happened at a car-manufacturer when their new CEO dropped his support halfway through the change: no fun for anyone at all.

In every case I've seen, full implementation of a service-oriented enterprise has brought real success to that organization, but as enterprise-architects responsible for key parts of that change, we must never underestimate the politics-issues involved in getting there…

## Summary

In this chapter, we explored the kinds of questions that we need to ask in order to create a service that will work effectively and reliably in real-world practice. The practical purpose of a service is to get something done – it *delivers* a service of some kind to the customer or consumer of that service. Practical concerns that arise from this include the need to ask what the service does, how it does so, and how the various functions and services are coordinated into a seamless business-process that provides the final service that the customer receives.

In the next, final chapter, we'll review what's needed in order to enhance, adapt, improve, and optimize our services within the ever-changing context of the service-oriented enterprise.

# CHAPTER 14

# Practice – Optimizing Services

Another of the architectural concerns arising from a technology-centered approach to service-architecture is that almost all of the attention is on service-execution and service-choreography, with little left over to assess what happens next. The service may be complete at that point from the requester's perspective, but not to the service-provider; there's often still a fair amount of work that needs to be done after the nominal service-request ends.

The first of these is the provision of the service-performance records required by the parent management-service. They may not seem relevant to the service itself, but they *are* indeed needed for overall resource-management and service-coordination. And then later – sometimes quite a lot later – there will need to be an audit to verify the performance-information coming up the hierarchy-tree. More precisely, there needs to be at least one audit-process for *each* of the core-values of the enterprise that are monitored by the pervasive-services – and performance-metrics to match those values, too.

If those audits don't take place, there's almost no point in defining the respective values, because there would be no way to ensure that the enterprise is "on track" toward its vision, role, missions, or goals. And they need to pervade *every* part of the enterprise – which means that the audits need to apply to *every* service, all the way down to the manual processes and the detail-level IT.

© Tom Graves 2023
T. Graves, *The Service-Oriented Enterprise*, https://doi.org/10.1007/978-1-4842-9189-4_14

If we can't measure it, we can't manage it. And if we can't manage it, we can't improve it either. Those audits *matter*.

# Application Themes: Audit to Improve

- What audit-processes already exist for the services in your enterprise? What concerns and values are audited, and for what purposes?

- What performance-information is passed up the hierarchy-tree from each service? If this information passes through various transforms and aggregations on its way up the tree, by what means can the original source-information be identified and audited?

- By what architectural means can you ensure that performance-metrics are garnered for *every* enterprise core-value? By what means can you ensure that such information is collected in formats that are amenable to subsequent audit?

- In what ways is performance-information – as verified via audit – reused and reapplied in the improvement-processes of the enterprise? In what parts of the enterprise, and for what services, do these respective improvement-processes apply?

- What audit-information and audit-processes are used to verify each instance of intended improvement?

- Where multiple implementations exist for a single service – such as for disaster-recovery or load-balancing – by what means can you ensure that the same overall audit-processes and audit-criteria apply to all implementations?

- What information-gaps and audit-gaps exist in the enterprise? If any, in what areas and at what levels of the enterprise do those gaps occur? What can you do to resolve those gaps, in terms of the service-architecture, service-designs, and service implementations?

The audit is also the last stage of the pervasive-services' own improvement-cycle of develop awareness, develop-capability, execution, and audit, which maintain momentum toward an ever-improving expression of the enterprise values. In its way, this is much the same as the Deming/Shewhart quality-improvement cycle of *plan, do, check, act,* with develop-awareness as "plan," develop-capability as "do," the audit of task-execution itself as "check," and the follow-up to the audit as "act." So there needs to be quite a strong cross-reference between the pervasive-services and the "change the business" coordination-services that guide the planned changes to the service-catalogue, the service-choreographies, and the services themselves.

# Improvement and Optimization

Perhaps the most important part of any improvement-cycle – and the part that turns it into a *cycle,* rather than a linear goal-based sequence – is the "lessons-learned" process that occurs after all the nominal is complete. In the TOGAF ADM enterprise architecture methodology, for example, there's a "Phase H" review-phase that occurs at the end of the architecture-iteration; in the Deming cycle, it's the "check" phase, leading to the "act" analysis that starts a new cycle. One of the simplest yet most effective techniques for this is the US Army's "After Action Review," which consists of just four questions:

- *"What was supposed to happen?"* – "plan"

- *"What actually happened?"* – "do"

- *"What was the source of the difference?"* – "check"

- *"What can we learn from this, to do better next time?"* – "act"

That whole review-process can be done in as little as a matter of minutes. In general, you should aim to spend perhaps a quarter of the time on the first two questions, another quarter on the third question, and half the time on the last. There are also two firm rules for the review: "no blame" and "pin your stripes at the door." We need the "no blame" rule because the moment that blame starts flying around, no-one's going to learn anything. And we need "pin your stripes at the door" because, for this kind of review to work well, everyone must be considered equal, regardless of any nominal rank, and no-one has priority over anyone else; everyone had their job to do, their own responsibilities, and the aim is for *everyone* to find out how to do their work better, both individually and as a collective team.

In a service-architecture context, we might apply much the same principles to review how we model patterns of "completeness" or "incompleteness"; the recursion of patterns in service-structures; the trade-offs between abstract services and their real implementations in "normal" business-processes, and for abnormal conditions such as disaster-recovery; or other trade-offs, such as optimization of service transactions. If each of those is the plan – "what was supposed to happen?" – then what did the service actually do? What caused the difference between intention, expectation, and real-world result? What can we learn from this? That's what this type of review would explore.

The specific content of the review doesn't matter that much here; what *does* matter is that some kind of lessons-learned review must take place immediately after the action is over, and that the results of those reviews should feed back into service-improvement.

## Application Themes: Lessons-Learned

- What "lessons-learned" processes exist for the enterprise-architecture, and for services in general throughout the enterprise?

- What is learned from such reviews? In what ways do you act on the "lessons learned"?

- By what means do the results of such lessons-learned reviews feed back into the "change the business" coordination-services? How would you verify that those results have been applied – and applied appropriately – within the change-processes?

Another point here is that this is also a *social* process, in which the context is viewed from multiple levels and multiple perspectives. It's not the machine-metaphor's rigid separation between "brawnless brain" and "brainless brawn"; we make full use of experience and knowledge from *every* aspect of the context to identify and apply those "lessons learned." So while the architecture for a service-oriented enterprise will involve a great deal of analysis, of *thinking* and suchlike, it's also necessarily a social process of engagement with each of the service's stakeholders. To create the *effectiveness* that we need across the entire enterprise, optimization depends upon that process of engagement.

# Optimization and Engagement

An enterprise is a social community, sharing a common purpose. And social communities operate – or literally *co*-operate – through mutual service. So service isn't just some "nice idea" for academics; it's a key survival-strategy in any fast-changing ecosystem. Service-orientation *matters*.

If the sense of service is a desirable core-value for the enterprise, and a service-orientation is a desirable outcome for that value, then service-oriented architecture itself implicitly is, and needs to be, one of the pervasive-services for the enterprise. This means that a key part of architecture work must revolve around engaging people in the *practical* expression of the value of services: creating awareness of that value; developing capability to support it; verifying that that value is in real everyday use, guiding decision-making throughout the enterprise; and taking action to enhance it wherever practicable, again throughout the enterprise. A service-oriented architecture doesn't sit in one place, hidden away in the enterprise equivalent of an ivory tower: it's *everywhere*. Engagement *is* the architecture.

Describing the detailed processes needed for architectural engagement would require a book in itself, but fortunately we don't have to do that, because the information we need already exists elsewhere, in practical research on change-management, knowledge-management, and so on. Some recommended sources include

- Knowledge-sharing within large organizations, such as described by Collison and Parcell, and many others

- Knowledge-sharing through "communities of practice," such as described by Etienne Wenger and his colleagues

- Narrative knowledge and "business storytelling," such as described by Shawn Callahan and others at the Australian consultancy Anecdote

- Developing and sustaining a proactive, self-adapting "learning organization," such as described by Peter Senge and colleagues

The knowledge needed for optimization of services is distributed throughout the enterprise; engagement in architecture is one of the key means by which the enterprise can access that knowledge from within itself.

# Application Themes: Architecture Engagement

- What processes and tools do you use to engage stakeholders in the various stages of the architecture process – particularly the review-phases?

- How do you publish and promulgate the results of your work at present? What architecture artifacts do you produce?

- What mechanisms exist to garner and incorporate feedback into the architecture? What can you do to make that happen and to verify the quality of what happens?

- What support does your existing architecture-toolset provide in this? If any exists, is it broadcast-only, does it allow feedback via annotation, or is it fully bidirectional?

- How do you measure the effectiveness of architecture? How is the business-value of the architecture itself identified and measured? What metrics are used for this? What improvements could be made in those metrics, and in the ways in which they are gathered, reviewed, and reused?

- What metrics are used to measure the value of the overall enterprise? In what terms are those metrics defined? To what extent do they align with the espoused vision and values of the enterprise? If the alignment is poor, what could you do in architectural terms to improve it?

- What else could you do to enhance awareness and engagement by the enterprise in its own architecture?

In the end, the real driver here – the real "desirable value" – is to improve enterprise *effectiveness*: improved efficiency, reliability, clarity, and simplicity, everything "on purpose," everything and everyone working together toward the common aims. Service-oriented architecture and an overall service-orientation for the enterprise will definitely help in this endeavor. As an enterprise architect, how much of that ideal may be fulfilled is ultimately up to you.

# Summary

In this chapter, we explored the importance of audits and reviews to close the loop for continual improvement in services, and how to make that happen. From the customer's perspective, the service ends once the results specified in the service-contract have been delivered. But for the service-provider, there's a need for a final phase to review what has been done, and how well it has been done – and what else could be done to improve the overall effectiveness of the service-oriented enterprise.

# APPENDIX A

# Glossary

This section summarizes some of the key terms and acronyms used in the book.

| | |
|---|---|
| *appropriate* | Matching the intended overall purpose; a *REAL/LEARN* effectiveness-assessment theme associated with the *aspirational dimension* of the context |
| *aspirational dimension* | Aspirational and intentional aspects of work and the workplace, expressed in collective and individual identity and purpose, and in issues such as ethics, values, and codes of conduct; also commitment-assets and aspirational capital such as organizational morale, health, and fitness |
| *conceptual dimension* | Mental and conceptual aspects of work and the workspace: beliefs, attitudes, knowledge, procedures, and process specifications; also knowledge-assets and intellectual capital |
| *effective* | "On purpose," producing the intended overall result with an *optimized* balance over the whole; requires broad generalist awareness of the whole, rather than the narrow focus required to create local efficiency, hence often contrasted with *efficient*; see also *REAL/LEARN* |

(*continued*)

© Tom Graves 2023
T. Graves, *The Service-Oriented Enterprise*, https://doi.org/10.1007/978-1-4842-9189-4

| | |
|---|---|
| *efficient* | "Doing more with less," creating the maximum result with minimum use or wastage of resources in a specific activity or context; improved incrementally through *active learning* and related techniques for feedback and reflection, although major improvements usually require a change in paradigm; a *REAL/LEARN* theme associated with the *conceptual dimension* of the context |
| *elegant* | Human dimensions of *effectiveness*, such as feelings, emotions, and ergonomics, expressed in issues such as usability, simplicity, and personal preference; a *REAL/LEARN* effectiveness-assessment theme associated with the *relational dimension* of the context |
| *emergence* | Context within which cause-effect patterns can be identified only retrospectively, and in which analytic techniques are usually unreliable and misleading |
| *enterprise architecture* | A systematic process to model and guide *integration* and *optimization* of the entire enterprise |
| *FEAF* | Acronym for Federal Enterprise Architecture Framework, a framework and methodology developed for *enterprise architecture* by the US government |
| *goal* | A specific objective to be achieved by a specified point in time; emphasis on the behavioral or *physical dimension* of *purpose*, contrasted with *mission*, *role*, and *vision* |
| *integration* | Contextual awareness of all the interactions between the *physical*, *conceptual*, *relational*, and *aspirational* dimensions of work, and the workspace and the active process of linking them together into a unified whole |
| *mission* | A desired capability or state to be achieved, usually within a specified timeframe, and to be maintained indefinitely once achieved; emphasis on the *emotional* and, to a lesser extent, the *conceptual dimensions* of *purpose*, contrasted with *goal*, *role*, and *vision* |

*(continued)*

| | |
|---|---|
| *narrative* | Personalized and often emotive expression or interpretation of knowledge, as history, anecdote, or story; link-theme between *mental dimension* and *relational dimension* |
| *optimization* | Process of *integration* in which *efficiency* in different areas is traded-off and balanced for maximum *effectiveness* over the whole, between different layers and subcontexts such as departments, business processes, and business units |
| *physical dimension* | Physical aspects of work and the workspace: skills, competencies, physical processes, behaviors, actions; also tangible assets and work-environment |
| *principle* | A conceptual or aspirational commitment or model, the *conceptual-dimension* or *aspirational-dimension* equivalent of *value* |
| *purpose* | An expression of individual and/or collective identity – the *aspirational* theme of "who we are and what we stand for"; incorporates distinct dimensions of *vision, role, mission*, and *goal* |
| $R^5$ | Collective term for five complexity-science principles used with the *tetradian*, namely, *recursion, rotation, reflexion, reciprocation*, and *resonance* |
| *REAL/LEARN* | Acronym for four keywords to evaluate effectiveness: reliable, efficient, appropriate, elegant; the LEARN acronym includes *integration* in the evaluation-set |
| *reciprocation* | Overall balance in transactions, especially *power*-transactions; reciprocal balance between entities may not be direct or immediate, and in many cases balance may only be achieved over time at a system-wide level, with energy-transfers occurring between *physical, conceptual, relational*, and/or *aspirational* dimensions; an $R^5$ principle for assessment of *effectiveness* and relevance |

(*continued*)

| | |
|---|---|
| *recursion* | Patterns of relationship or interaction repeat or are "self-similar" at different scales; permits simplification of otherwise complex processes; an $R^5$ principle for assessment of *effectiveness* and relevance |
| *reflexion* | Corollary of *recursion*, in that the whole, or aspects of the whole, can be identified within the attributes and transactions of any part at any scale; an $R^5$ principle for assessment of *effectiveness* and relevance |
| *relational dimension* | Relational and emotional aspects of the work context: feelings and *values*, internal relationships and interpersonal transactions, relationships with external stakeholders; also assets such as reputation and trust |
| *reliable* | High degree of certainty and predictability for a desired outcome; a *REAL/LEARN* effectiveness-assessment theme associated with the *physical dimension* of the context |
| *resonance* | Concept of positive-or negative-feedback (increasing or damping) in a system; permits simplification of otherwise complex processes; an $R^5$ principle for assessment of *effectiveness* and relevance |
| *rotation* | Systematic process of assessing a context from multiple perspectives; an $R^5$ principle for assessment of *effectiveness* and relevance |
| *role* | A declared focus or *strategic* position within the "world" described by a *vision*; emphasis on the *conceptual* and, to a lesser extent, the *relational dimensions* of *purpose*, contrasted with *goal*, *mission*, and *vision* |
| *scenario* | An imagined future context, developed for the purpose of understanding both the present context and options for action in the future context |

(*continued*)

| | |
|---|---|
| *strategy* | "Big picture" view of an action-plan for an organization to implement a *purpose*, usually emphasizing its *vision, role*, and *mission* components; contrasted with the *tactics* required to execute the plan |
| *tactics* | Detailed *missions, goals*, and other step-by-step activities to execute a *strategy*, or some segment of an overall strategy |
| *tetradian* | Depiction of the *physical, conceptual, relational*, and *aspirational* dimensions of a context as four axes in a tetrahedral relationship, usually also showing the respective link-themes as the edges between the vertices of the tetrahedron |
| *TOGAF* | Acronym for The Open Group Architecture Framework, an IT-oriented framework and methodology for *enterprise architecture* developed collectively by members of the Open Group consortium |
| *value* | An emotional commitment |
| *vision* | Description of a desired "world," always far greater than any individual or organization; described in the present tense, yet is never "achieved"; emphasis on the *aspirational dimension* of *purpose*, contrasted with *goal, mission*, and *role*; also link-theme between *aspirational dimension* and *relational dimension* |
| *visioning* | Generic term for the process of identifying, developing, and documenting *vision* and *values*, leading toward *strategy* and *tactics* |
| *Zachman framework* | A systematic structure for categorization of models within an IT-oriented *enterprise architecture*, developed by John Zachman |

# APPENDIX B

# Resources

## Books

Stafford Beer, *Brain of the Firm* (Allen Lane: The Penguin Press, 1972)

Chris Collison and Geoff Parcell, *Learning to Fly: practical lessons from one of the world's leading knowledge companies* (Capstone, 2001)

Arie de Geus, *The Living Company* (Longview Publishing, 1997)

Tom Graves, *Real Enterprise Architecture: beyond IT to the whole enterprise* (Tetradian, 2008)

Tom Graves, *Bridging the Silos: enterprise architecture for IT-architects* (Tetradian, 2008)

Tom Graves, *Power and Response-ability: the human side of systems* (Tetradian, 2008)

Tom Graves, *SEMPER and SCORE: enhancing enterprise effectiveness* (Tetradian, 2008)

Tom Graves, "The Viable Services Model: Service quality, service interdependence and service completeness" in Jan van Bon [ed.], *IT Service Management: Global best practices* (itSMF/Van Haren, 2008)

Nigel Green and Carl Bate, *Lost In Translation: a handbook for information systems in the 21st century* (Evolved Media, 2007)

Charles Handy, *Beyond Certainty* (Arrow Books, 1996)

Kees van der Heijden, *Scenarios: the art of strategic conversation* (Wiley, 2004)

© Tom Graves 2023
T. Graves, *The Service-Oriented Enterprise*, https://doi.org/10.1007/978-1-4842-9189-4

Michael Henderson and Dougal Thompson, *Values At Work: the invisible threads between people, performance and profit* (HarperBusiness New Zealand, 2003)

Patrick Hoverstadt, *The Fractal Organization: Creating sustainable organizations with the Viable System Model* (Wiley, 2008)

Sohail Inayatullah [ed.], *The Causal Layered Analysis (CLA) Reader: theory and case studies of an integrative and transformative methodology* (Taipei: Tamkang University Press, 2004)

RS Kaplan and DP Norton, *Balanced Scorecard: Translating Strategy into Action* (Harvard Business School Press, 1996)

Whynde Kuehn, *Strategy to Reality: Making the impossible possible for business architects, change makers and strategy execution leaders* (Morgan James Publishing, 2022)

Suzanne Robertson and James Robertson, *Mastering the Requirements Process* (Addison-Wesley, 1999)

Jeanne W. Ross, Peter Weill and David Robertson, *Enterprise Architecture As Strategy: Creating a Foundation for Business Execution* (Harvard Business Press, 2008)

Peter Senge, *The Fifth Discipline: The Art & Practice of the Learning Organization* (Doubleday, 1990)

Peter Senge, *The Dance of Change: The Challenges of Sustaining Momentum in Learning Organizations* (Nicholas Brealey Publishing, 1999)

Etienne Wenger, Richard McDermott and William M. Snyder, *Cultivating Communities of Practice: a guide to managing knowledge* (Harvard Business School Press, 2002)

# Online Resources

Activity-based costing: see Wikipedia summary at en.wikipedia.org/wiki/Activity-based_costing

After-action review: see Wikipedia summary at en.wikipedia.org/wiki/After-action_review

Agile architecture development: see www.bcs.org/articles-opinion-and-research/what-is-agile-enterprise-architecture/

Balanced scorecard: see Wikipedia summary at en.wikipedia.org/wiki/Balanced_scorecard

Beer Game: see beergame.org/the-game/

BiSL (Business Information Services Library) and ASL (Application Services Library): see www.didfoundation.com/

Business Motivation Model: see businessrulesgroup.org/bmm.htm

Business Process Model and Notation (BPMN): see www.bpmn.org/ and Wikipedia summary at en.wikipedia.org/wiki/Business_Process_Model_and_Notation

Causal Layered Analysis: see www.metafuture.org/Articles/CausalLayeredAnalysis.htm

Cybersyn project, Chile, 1971–1973: see Wikipedia summary at en.wikipedia.org/wiki/Project_Cybersyn

Deming/Shewhart "Plan, Do, Check, Act" cycle: see Wikipedia summary at en.wikipedia.org/wiki/PDCA

Enhanced Telecom Operations Map (eTOM): see Wikipedia summary at en.wikipedia.org/wiki/ETOM

Environmental scanning for business context: see Wikipedia summary at en.wikipedia.org/wiki/Environmental_scanning

Etienne Wenger on "communities of practice": see www.wenger-trayner.com/etienne/

FEAF (US Federal Enterprise Architecture Framework): see Wikipedia summary at en.wikipedia.org/wiki/Federal_enterprise_architecture

Frederick Taylor and "scientific management": see Wikipedia summary at en.wikipedia.org/wiki/Scientific_management

Future Search: see futuresearch.net

ITIL (Information Technology Infrastructure Library): see www.itil.org.uk and Wikipedia summary at en.wikipedia.org/wiki/ITIL

Narrative knowledge and business-storytelling: see www.anecdote.com

Open Space Technology: see Wikipedia summary at en.wikipedia.org/wiki/Open_Space_Technology

Principles of "living enterprise": see naomistanford.com/organisations-as-living-systems/

Ray Anderson and the Interface, Inc. story: see Wikipedia biography at en.wikipedia.org/wiki/Ray_Anderson_(entrepreneur) and `www.greenbiz.com/article/20-years-later-interface-looks-back-ray-andersons-legacy`

Service-oriented IT-architecture: see Wikipedia summary at en.wikipedia.org/wiki/Service-oriented_architecture

Supply-Chain Operations Reference model (SCOR): see Wikipedia summary at en.wikipedia.org/wiki/Supply_chain_operations_reference

TOGAF (The Open Group Architecture Framework): see opengroup.org/togaf

Tuckman "Group Dynamics": see Wikipedia summary at en.wikipedia.org/wiki/Tuckman%27s_stages_of_group_development

Unified Modeling Language (UML): see `www.uml.org` and Wikipedia summary at en.wikipedia.org/wiki/Unified_Modeling_Language

Viable system model: see Wikipedia summary at en.wikipedia.org/wiki/Viable_system_model

W Edwards Deming and quality: see Wikipedia summary at en.wikipedia.org/wiki/W._Edwards_Deming

Zachman framework: see Wikipedia summary at en.wikipedia.org/wiki/Zachman_Framework

# Index

Printed in the United States
by Baker & Taylor Publisher Services